A Very Merry *Holiday* Movie Guide

Rachel McMillan

ARTWORK BY LAURA L. BEAN

HARVEST HOUSE PUBLISHERS
EUGENE, OREGON

Cover design by Studio Gearbox
Interior design by Dugan Design Group
Published in association with William K. Jensen Literary Agency

A Very Merry Holiday Movie Guide

Published by Harvest House Publishers
Eugene, Oregon 97408
www.harvesthousepublishers.com

ISBN 978-0-7369-8171-2 (pbk.)
ISBN 978-0-7369-8172-9 (eBook)

Library of Congress Cataloging-in-Publication Data record is available at
https://lccn.loc.gov/2020018521

Printed in the United States of America

20 21 22 23 24 25 26 27 28 / VP-DDG / 10 9 8 7 6 5 4 3 2 1

Contents

INTRODUCTION

Confessions of a Christmas-Movie Addict

I like to say I found them first, long before so many viewers began tuning in to the dozens of new made-for-TV Christmas offerings produced every year.

When I was on medical leave from my corporate job one fall, my channel surfing stopped on a showing of ***Secret Santa***, a 2003 Hallmark Christmas movie starring Jennie Garth as a reporter trying to discover the identity of a small-town do-gooder—and finding love in the bargain.

It was only mid-November, but the Christmas movie lineup didn't stop there. From ***Lucky Christmas*** to ***November Christmas*** to ***Holiday in Handcuffs***, I found a series of warm hugs during a trying time, retreating into a snow-globe world of love and gingerbread houses.

Christmas has always been a passion of mine. As a little girl, I begged my minister father to have the congregation start singing carols as early as November 1 (sadly, my plea didn't work), and I lined up my teddy bears and dolls for a Happy Birthday, Jesus party in the middle of August. So the traditions, music, snow, and tinsel I had always loved and now found in those films comforted me. No matter what I was feeling on any given day, I could always return to a safe world where the most difficult concern was whether there would be snow by Christmas or the town's cookie factory would find a last-minute benefactor on Christmas Eve. (Spoiler alert: snow always appears by the end of the movie, and the factory will always be saved. In a world of uncertainty, a Christmas movie ends happily, without fail.)

These movies became my friends, and I soon learned that they were broadcast again and again in between new offerings launched every year as early as October 1 and through Epiphany in early January.

From that autumn onward, I discovered Christmas movies could calm me and give me a warm glow even through family health scares, after challenging days at work, during illness, or just when experiencing a case of the blues. I never leave home without a digital copy of ***A Very Merry Mix-Up*** downloaded on my laptop *in case of emergency*.

But I'm not the only one who loves these films. In the last five years especially, this genre has become a cultural phenomenon—with what seems like at least 90 percent of the North American population tuning in. Channels such as Hallmark, UP TV, ABC Spark, and Lifetime produce dozens of new holiday movies every single year. Now streaming services like Netflix and Amazon Prime have followed suit. Major publications such as *Cosmopolitan*, the *Washington Post*, *Entertainment Weekly*, and *NPR* have studied this trend that finds G-rated TV series, such as **When Calls the Heart**, and the latest Candace Cameron Bure or Lacey Chabert Christmas film rivaling broadcast networks, including HBO and AMC. Today, the launch of a new holiday-themed flick airing as early as October 26 can garner nearly 40 million viewers.

People love these predictable festive movies because they provide what daily life in our tumultuous world cannot: a feeling of wholesome goodness and consistent portrayals of values, hope, and faith. We know love will always win and goodwill will always prevail. We know the rising corporate marketing star sent to her hometown to spy on the local hat factory at Christmas will choose the honest and hardworking community she finds there rather than the trappings of posh clothes and the penthouse apartment she inhabits in the big city. Christmas movies are *every good and pure thing* lacking in a culture determined to scorn morals, traditional values, family ties, and the hope of chaste, true love.

The viewing stats of these increasingly popular films say silently

With this opportunity to join in the world's collective love for such a Christmas, then, let's do it. Let's own it!

what society isn't saying aloud: For all of the contemporary focus on throwaway relationships and the love of money, greed, and materialism, a desire for the ideals of Christmas remains.

For a few months a year (not to mention most Friday nights and Hallmark's annual Christmas in July), everything is all right. The cookies are baked and decorated, the fire is roaring, the perfect Charlie Brown tree is selected from the neighborhood tree farm with the kind owner, the hot chocolate is rich, and the turkey is cooked.

With this opportunity to join in the world's collective love for such a Christmas, then, let's do it. Let's *own* it! Find the Christmas sweater you inherited from your great-aunt and add a few extra marshmallows to your hot chocolate. Make watching holiday movies you DVR year after year and the film premieres you've not yet seen special events and a tradition.

This book will help you do all that and more. It's a celebration of Christmas movies and Christmas movie lovers curated by a Christmas-loving woman who knows these made-for-TV films are one of the reasons we call the Christmas season the most wonderful time of the year, while also believing they can kick-start everything from tree decorating to cookie baking.

Start with the chapter that most clearly identifies your favorite aspect of the holiday. Unlike the repetitive song, there's no right or wrong way to approach Hallmark's 12 Days of Christmas Movies. Try out a few new film offerings and recipes. Establish fun new traditions with your family and friends. Designed as an emblem of everything we love about Christmas movies, this book will perhaps inspire you to get creative, become passionate, and be full of the holiday spirit as you play with its ideas and add some of your own movies and traditions to create Christmas memories you'll never forget.

Your Christmas Movie Lover's Kit

- flannel pj's or a festive onesie or robe
- Christmas-themed socks or slippers
- Santa hat or reindeer antlers
- a few favorite Christmas movie DVDs or the passwords to streaming service subscriptions
- hot chocolate mix packets; miniature marshmallows
- candy canes

Note: This package for yourself can also inspire a great gift for another Christmas movie lover in your life.

Your Christmas Bucket List

In the film ***The Christmas List***, Christmas lover Isobel makes a list of all of the Christmassy things she's always wanted to do but never taken time for. Making a list of your own with your family or a few friends is a great way to check off some of your must-do Christmas activities for the season, such as

- mailing Christmas cards to family and friends

- visiting a department store Santa and having your picture taken with a pet, your girlfriends, or, if you don't have little ones of your own, a niece, nephew, or godchild
- finding a local theater showing ***It's a Wonderful Life*** or ***White Christmas*** on the big screen
- attending an outdoor, living nativity pageant
- decorating a real tree chosen at a local tree farm instead of an artificial one
- taking a Christmas cookie baking class
- going ice skating at a local rink or safely frozen lake
- attending a church- or community-run Christmas craft bazaar
- finding a local stage production of ***A Christmas Carol***
- taking a wagon or sleigh ride at a community farm or orchard

Note: ***The Christmas List*** (2016) is based on the novella *The Christmas Bucket List* by Ella Fairlie, which has even more ideas for a prospective list of your own.

A Guide for Beginning Christmas Movie Viewers

- If you have the Hallmark Movies and Mysteries Channel or Hallmark Channel, download their yearly Christmas app so you can check for new films you haven't seen as well as what movies you would like to revisit.

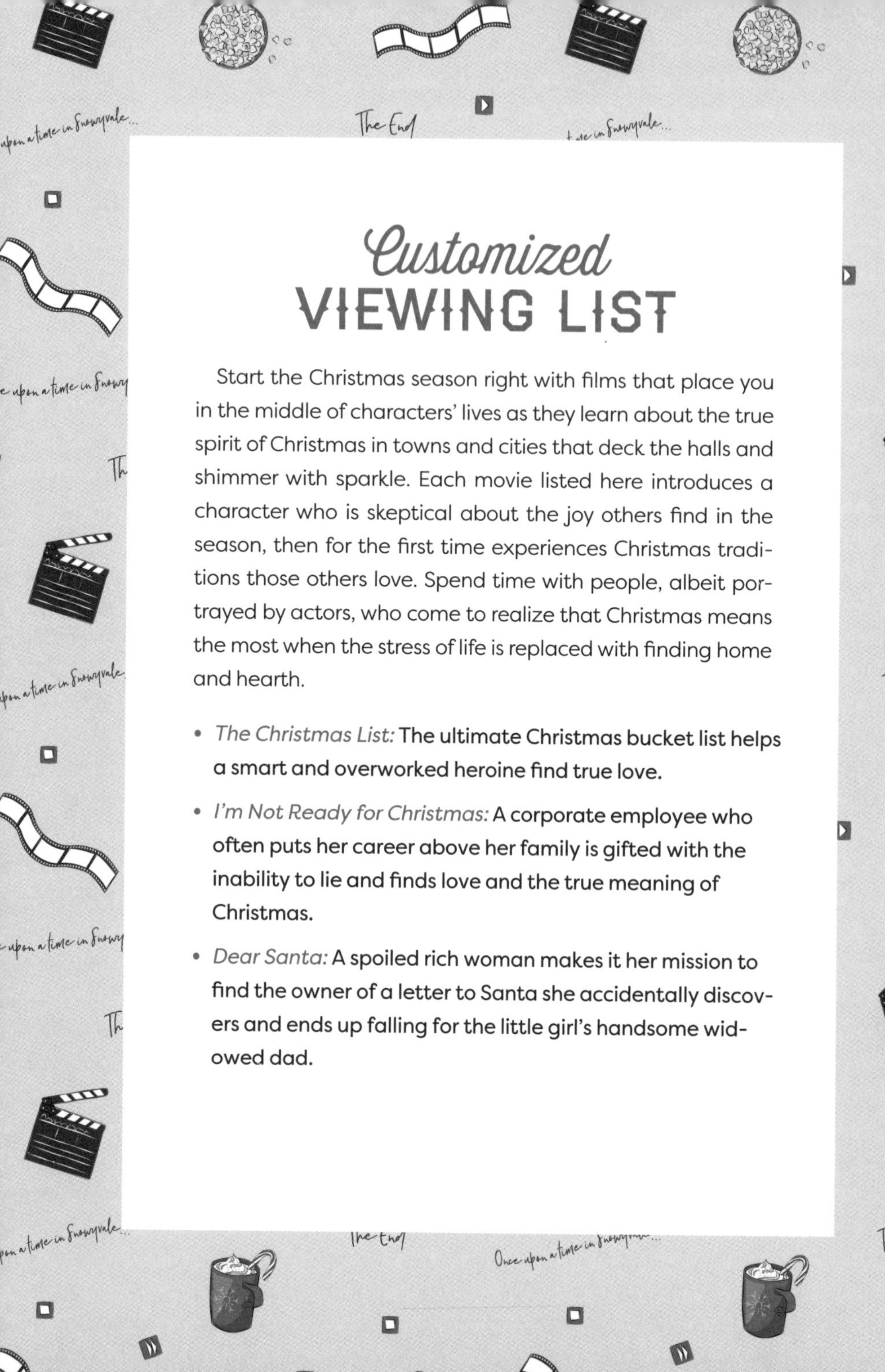

Customized VIEWING LIST

Start the Christmas season right with films that place you in the middle of characters' lives as they learn about the true spirit of Christmas in towns and cities that deck the halls and shimmer with sparkle. Each movie listed here introduces a character who is skeptical about the joy others find in the season, then for the first time experiences Christmas traditions those others love. Spend time with people, albeit portrayed by actors, who come to realize that Christmas means the most when the stress of life is replaced with finding home and hearth.

- *The Christmas List:* The ultimate Christmas bucket list helps a smart and overworked heroine find true love.
- *I'm Not Ready for Christmas:* A corporate employee who often puts her career above her family is gifted with the inability to lie and finds love and the true meaning of Christmas.
- *Dear Santa:* A spoiled rich woman makes it her mission to find the owner of a letter to Santa she accidentally discovers and ends up falling for the little girl's handsome widowed dad.

- *Christmas in Evergreen: Letters to Santa:* A small town full of old-fashioned values and Dear Santa letters provides the perfect opportunity for viewers to settle into a Currier and Ives printlike setting.
- *Switched for Christmas:* Twins swap lives for the holiday season and get more than they bargain for in both life and love.

- Check both your local library and your church library for Christmas movie DVDs you can borrow.
- Start a collection of your own Christmas DVDs by shopping after-Christmas sales on Amazon or at Target or Walmart. Three or four films are often packaged in one DVD.
- Check web and streaming services:
    - Netflix produces their own Christmas movies.
    - Amazon Prime has several made-for-TV Christmas movies as well as classics.
    - iTunes has made-for-TV Christmas movies as well as theatrical releases for rent and purchase.
    - Hulu carries a stream of Christmas movies.
    - Hallmark has a subscription streaming service that allows access to new films and old favorites.
- Search online for local listings on the following networks, which all produce new Christmas films every year:
    - ABC Spark
    - Lifetime
    - UP TV Network
    - Hallmark
    - Hallmark Movies and Mysteries
    - Disney

Setting the Movie-Watching Scene

One cannot thoroughly enjoy favorite made-for-TV Christmas movies with the same ambience in which one watches movies during any other season.

Christmas comes only once a year, so make it special.

- Set your ringtone to a favorite Christmas ditty, so even if you're movie watching is disturbed by a call, at least it will come with festive sounds.
- Make a fire in your fireplace—or throw up a YouTube loop of a fire in a fireplace on your laptop if you don't have a fireplace. Either way, ensure the stockings are hung by the chimney—real or imagined—with care.
- Use candles or air fresheners to create a Christmassy scent or, alternatively, create your own scent. Fill a saucepan with a bit of water and simmer your favorite scents on medium heat. Apples, cloves, cinnamon, and oranges make for a mouth-watering, festive atmosphere throughout your home (but don't forget to turn off the stove). Pine branches in a bit of water can make your house smell like a real Christmas tree even if you've opted for an artificial one to avoid having to vacuum fallen needles.

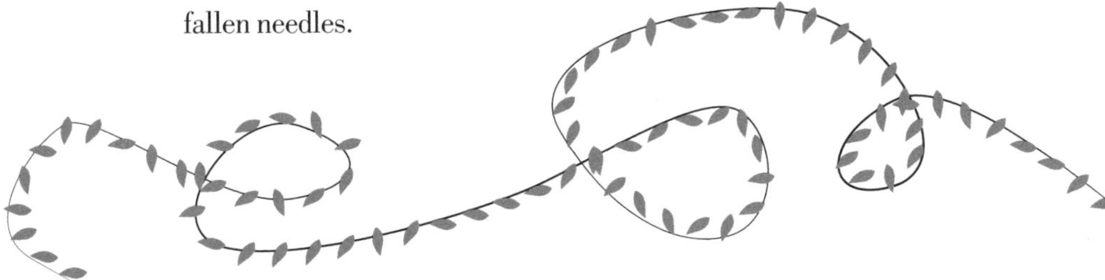

Discover Your Christmas Movie Name

Unless your name, like the names of so many made-for-TV heroines, is already Christmassy, give yourself a movie name by pairing two words, one from each of the two columns below.

THE FIRST LETTER OF YOUR FIRST NAME		YOUR BIRTH MONTH	
A–D	Merry	Jan–Feb	Kringle
E–H	Ivy	March–April	Silver
I–M	Joy	May–June	Gold
N–Q	Belle	July–August	St. Nicholas
R–U	Angel	Sep–October	Pine
V–Z	Holly	Nov–Dec	Evergreen

Make Reindeer Trail Mix

Let's face it, Christmas is a challenging time to eat healthfully. But enjoying stewed apples or pears with brown sugar, fresh clementine orange slices, or even trail mix is a step in the right direction. And with all of that sleigh-pulling, Rudolph and his eight friends more than need some protein.

- Choose a two-nut base. Almonds, peanuts, walnuts, or cashews are a great start.
- Add a favorite dried cereal, such as Chex or Shredded Wheat.
- Add some favorite dried fruit. Cranberries, raisins, and bananas are all wonderful!
- Mix in red and green M&M's to perfect a sweet and salty balance. They're also great with popcorn.

Embrace This Eggnog Tip

Do you love eggnog but find the taste too rich? Add a dash of it to tea or coffee in lieu of cream or milk.

Create a Hot Chocolate Bar

To accommodate everyone's cocoa tastes, put out bowls of miniature marshmallows (colored ones can be festive!) and sprinkles, some canned whipped cream, cayenne pepper for those who like a kick, peppermint candy canes, and extra chocolate syrup .

Even when a lot of elves are enjoying the holiday together, they can all avoid picking up the wrong drink when everyone makes their own candy cane reindeer to hook in the handle of their mug of hot chocolate. Not only is this activity a fun icebreaker—or these can be party favors if you make them ahead of time—but it recalls the crafts many of us made as kids.

What you'll need:

- candy cane
- glue
- brown pipe cleaners
- craft-store googly eyes
- small red pompoms or candies

How to make one: Glue two eyes and a pompom or piece of candy for a nose to a candy cane and press tightly so the little pieces stick. Affix a pipe cleaner to the top of the candy cane, pressing and adjusting until you get the shape of antlers you like.

Start a New TRADITION

Christmas is a wonderful time for family and friends, but don't forget to make time for *your* movies and *your* Christmas experiences before you get caught up in the holiday bustle. Even if you get into the holiday season the moment the holiday films begin showing up on your favorite channels, though, the festive season can often pass by far too quickly. For one thing, some of the TV movies in your DVR might escape your attention as the season slips away or while you're just spending time with your beautiful decorations and some peace.

Right before Thanksgiving weekend, and taking note of your planned holiday events, schedule one evening or afternoon in the weeks leading to Christmas just for a designated "my Christmas time," wherein you celebrate and enjoy the season your own way. Watch one of your favorite made-for-TV Christmas movies from long ago (***A Very Merry Mix-Up*** is mine!) alongside hot chocolate and marshmallows. Window-shop for holiday decorations on foot or online. Read one of the many Christmas-themed books you've added to your Goodreads list since they released in September.

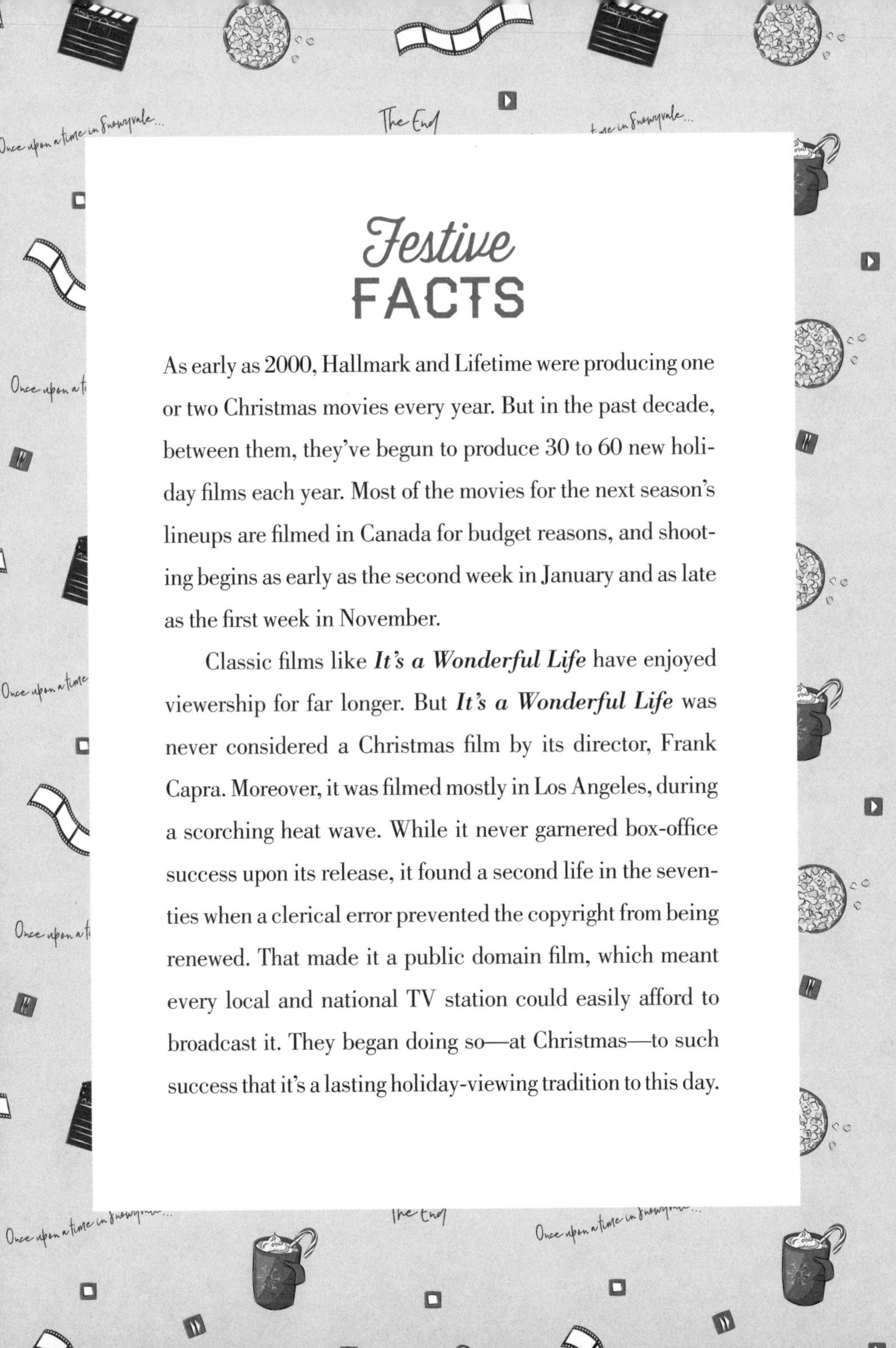

Festive FACTS

As early as 2000, Hallmark and Lifetime were producing one or two Christmas movies every year. But in the past decade, between them, they've begun to produce 30 to 60 new holiday films each year. Most of the movies for the next season's lineups are filmed in Canada for budget reasons, and shooting begins as early as the second week in January and as late as the first week in November.

Classic films like ***It's a Wonderful Life*** have enjoyed viewership for far longer. But ***It's a Wonderful Life*** was never considered a Christmas film by its director, Frank Capra. Moreover, it was filmed mostly in Los Angeles, during a scorching heat wave. While it never garnered box-office success upon its release, it found a second life in the seventies when a clerical error prevented the copyright from being renewed. That made it a public domain film, which meant every local and national TV station could easily afford to broadcast it. They began doing so—at Christmas—to such success that it's a lasting holiday-viewing tradition to this day.

The Baker's Christmas

Whatever happened between us,
don't take it out on Christmas!

CHRISTMAS ON MY MIND

One of my favorite objects in the world is my mom's recipe box. She's collected our family's favorite Christmas recipes on little cards stained not only with thumbprints and crayon scribbles but by time, and I know which cards will be taken out of their holding places once a year. From my Tante Sylvia's cheeseball; to recipes my late grandmother, my Oma, loved; to the shortbread and spinach dip; to the slow-cooker mulled cider that makes the house smell like Christmas, the aromas and tastes of our traditional Christmas treats prompt a sense of nostalgia in me. But they also provide a link to loved ones long gone.

Baking and Christmas treats are at the heart of holiday traditions for many people. Not only do they allow new generations to capture the spirit of their heritage, but they inspire community and activity, whether in cookie-baking contests, at company bake sales, or in making a perfect, personal gift. More still, they can promote spending time in the kitchen for all ages and far from the bustle of the everyday—with the added reward of a sweet treat at the end.

And yet as we re-create our Christmas goodies every year, I wonder how we can continue to incorporate new traditions as the generations of our families expand—to nieces and nephews, in-laws, and grandchildren. Perhaps when thinking about our favorite recipes, we can make room for new ones. I encourage every family to try a new recipe this Christmas.

A Tasty Holiday

The traditions of baking and cooking are a wonderful springboard into learning about other cultures and how they celebrate the holidays. For example, making latkes (potato pancakes) is a wonderful

way to talk to your family about the Jewish celebration of Hanukkah without misappropriating a sacred holiday tradition. The Hallmark film ***Hitched for the Holidays*** balances the festive traditions of a large Italian-American family as well as a Jewish family preparing for Hanukkah. The film ***Christmas in Rome*** talks about the Italian tradition of making Panettone, a sweet bread, as a hostess gift to be consumed after a large, shared meal.

In countries such as Austria and the Czech Republic, Christmas dinners look different from many consumed in North America, and they're often served on Christmas Eve. The tradition of Christmas carp served with potato salad is a mainstay. Learning about the traditions and import of food in other cultures is a wonderful way to open interesting discussions about the holidays.

Make a Gingerbread Station

In the film ***The Christmas List***, Isobel's list includes making a gingerbread house, and a station of festive items is available for her to decorate it. Whether you make the gingerbread for your house from scratch or supplement a store-bought kit with personal additions, making a gingerbread house is always a fun activity. And especially as an activity for children or a girls' night, making gingerbread structures or people is the perfect opportunity for everyone to get creative. Here's a thought: Instead of making a gingerbread house, what about making a Santa's village?

Gingerbread station must-haves:

- different colored sprinkles
- different colored gumdrops
- licorice, red and black
- candy canes, any flavor or color
- chocolate kisses
- shredded coconut for snow
- marshmallows and toothpicks for snow people

Treasure Your Christmas Recipes

Ensure that a new generation can continue Christmas traditions by asking each family member what recipe or treat they most associate with the holiday. Write out those recipes on new cards, then decorate and date them and create a Christmas Recipe Box. That will be a fantastic gift for extended family and friends who share in your annual Christmas practices, ensuring that those recipes are preserved. You might even want to make a box for each household represented in your family and circle of celebrating friends.

Host a family or neighborhood baking exchange using some of the recipes most treasured in your family.

The traditions of baking and cooking are a wonderful springboard into learning about other cultures and how they celebrate the holidays.

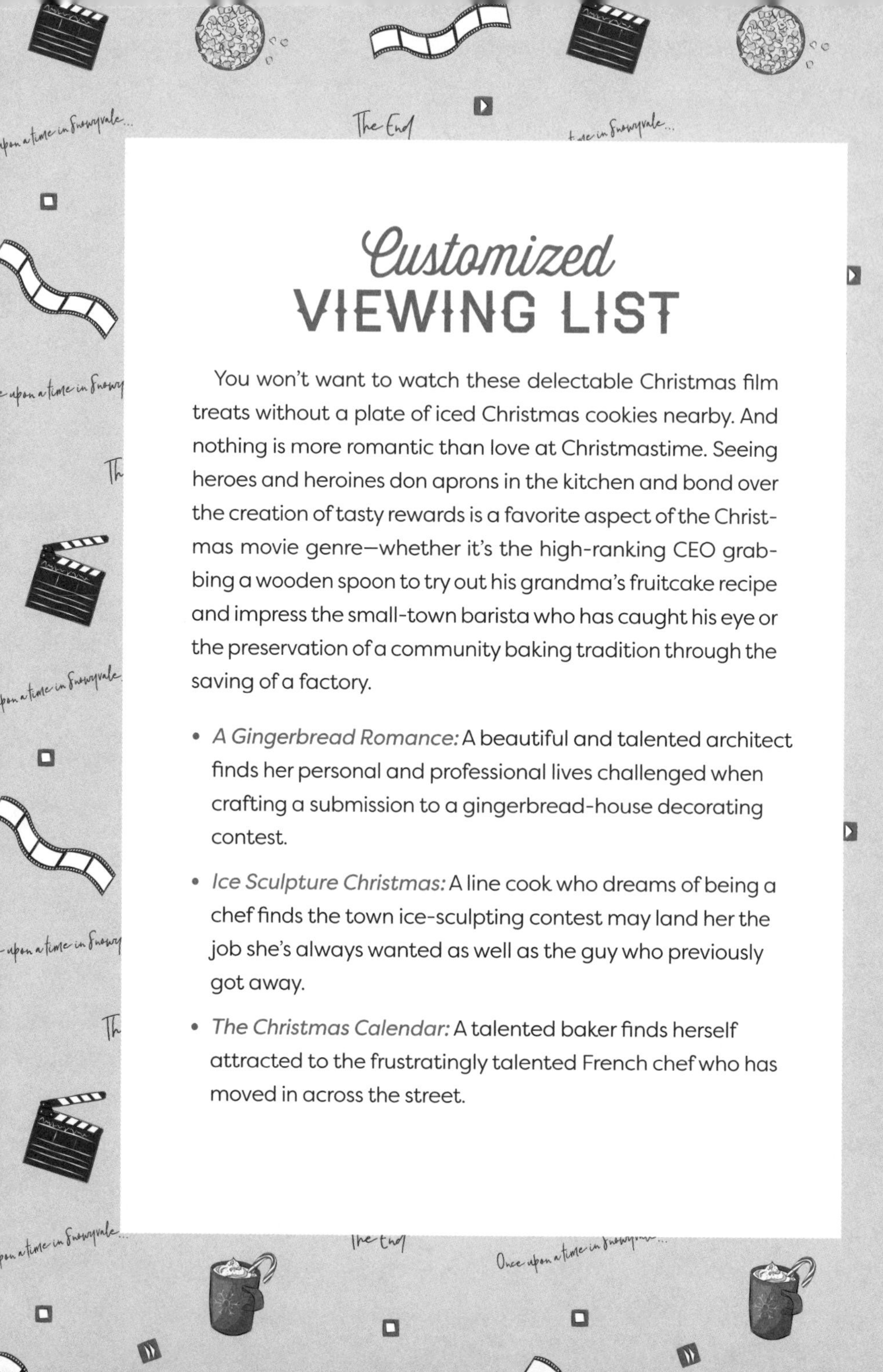

Customized VIEWING LIST

You won't want to watch these delectable Christmas film treats without a plate of iced Christmas cookies nearby. And nothing is more romantic than love at Christmastime. Seeing heroes and heroines don aprons in the kitchen and bond over the creation of tasty rewards is a favorite aspect of the Christmas movie genre—whether it's the high-ranking CEO grabbing a wooden spoon to try out his grandma's fruitcake recipe and impress the small-town barista who has caught his eye or the preservation of a community baking tradition through the saving of a factory.

- *A Gingerbread Romance:* A beautiful and talented architect finds her personal and professional lives challenged when crafting a submission to a gingerbread-house decorating contest.
- *Ice Sculpture Christmas:* A line cook who dreams of being a chef finds the town ice-sculpting contest may land her the job she's always wanted as well as the guy who previously got away.
- *The Christmas Calendar:* A talented baker finds herself attracted to the frustratingly talented French chef who has moved in across the street.

- *Merry & Bright:* Set in a historic candy cane manufacturing company, the successful CEO of Merry and Bright is closely watched by a visiting executive charged with studying the profitability of the struggling business.
- *A Cookie Cutter Christmas:* Two teachers use the school charity baking contest as a means of catching the eye of a handsome new single dad. But how far will the competition go?
- *Christmas Cookies:* A corporate agent is sent to a small town to shut down its famous cookie factory, then finds herself falling in love with the small-town traditions and the integrity of an old-fashioned company.

Your Emergency Midnight-Christmas-Cookie-Baking Checklist

What is a romantic Christmas movie without a midnight-cookie-baking spree? While ***Snowed-Inn Christmas*** finds two stranded reporters looking into the true nature of Christmas at an inn with owners who look surprisingly like everyone's favorite North Pole couple, so ***A Very Merry Mix-Up*** features a hero and heroine who, due to an unfortunate accident, need to stay awake for 24 hours straight! What better way to fall in love than among the aromas of Christmas baking?

In both cases, our beloved Christmas characters are supplied with a stocked kitchen ready for their middle-of-the-night raid. So in case a dashing would-be suitor arrives on your doorstep in the twilight hours during the holiday season, and whether you're snowed in together or you're merely swept off your feet, I suggest you stock your cupboards well in preparation for a possible baking session.

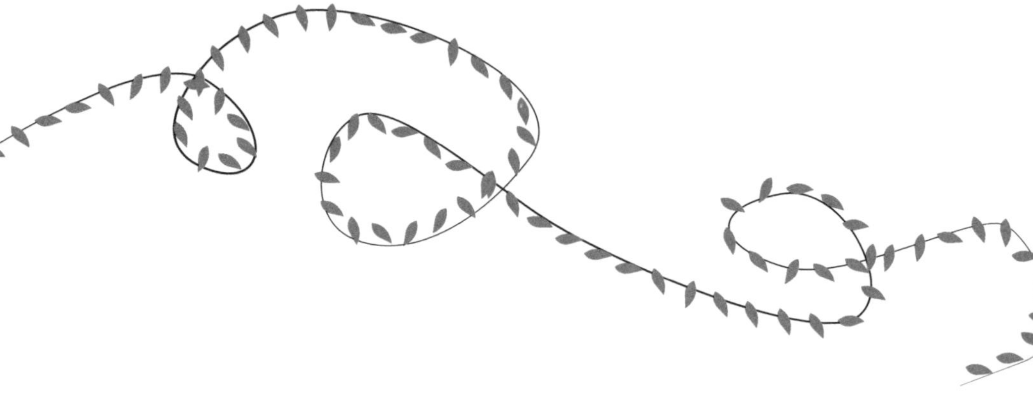

Here are some ways to ensure your kitchen is always midnight-baking ready at Christmas, even if you're alone:

- Keep holiday-themed cookie cutters at hand.
- Never be low on baking chocolate. (Not only does it work in a pinch for impromptu Christmas baking but eating some can be a lifesaver after a stressful day, no matter the season.)
- Flour, butter, sugar, and shortening are baking staples one must always have once Christmastime is here. Also make sure you have extra milk and eggs—especially if a snowstorm is on the way.

Start a New TRADITION

Advent calendars are one of my favorite parts of Christmas. Even today, my mom and dad still make sure I have a new one every year. But what might be more fun than using the U.S. Thanksgiving weekend to create an edible advent calendar with your family? Find a favorite candy or homemade chocolate recipe online and have the kids help decorate little envelopes or festive boxes, numbering each day. A wooden chest, plastic storage containers, or even a tiny Christmas tree are great ways to house your treats. Help make their efforts a surprise by organizing the goodies in random order and then mixing up the numbers.

Note: Hard candies, fudge, and homemade chocolates are probably the best nonperishable treats to feature in a homemade advent calendar. Either make these on your own or customize your Advent calendar by featuring some of the owner's favorite treats from a store.

Festive FACTS

Certain foods are staples of many Christmas celebrations—like turkey and gingerbread.

The tradition of eating turkey dates back to as early as sixteenth-century England, when turkeys were introduced to the country. Indeed, as the rumor goes, King Henry VIII was one of the first consumers of turkey on Christmas Day. Turkeys were a popular holiday bet because cows were needed for milking and chickens for their eggs. Though goose is a popular Christmas dish in many parts of the world, turkey-eating stuck.

Even Queen Elizabeth I supposedly created gingerbread men during her reign centuries later. But this goodie dates back to medieval times, when ginger, largely associated with medicinal purposes, was to be used for alternative purposes only on the most special of occasions. Today, gingerbread cookies and houses are among the most traditional treats enjoyed at Christmas.

The Shopper's Christmas

Well, I'm just not any stranger with a white beard, and this isn't just any red suit.

I'M NOT READY FOR CHRISTMAS

One of the many things I love about my favorite made-for-TV holiday movies is that the gifts at the center of the main relationships are meaningful: a lost heirloom, a found ornament, a tiny token from a high school sweetheart, a song composed and then performed next to the tree. I love the idea of meaningful gifts that cost little but time and heart. That being said, as the aunt of two little nieces and a nephew, I enjoy shopping for them much as I assume my aunts enjoyed shopping for me when I was small. The anticipation of giving someone a carefully selected gift you know they will love is as exciting as being on the receiving end.

If someone were to ask me my all-time favorite Christmas gift, I'd say it was the purple Precious Moments diary my brother, Jared, gave me when I was nine. Truthfully, my mom probably helped him choose it, because as kids, we all relied on her when it came to sibling gifts. I was so excited to have lined pages in a beautiful book to write in. That journal is definitely not the most extravagant or expensive gift I've received over the years, but it stands out in my memory and heart.

Another Christmas, I received copies of the books I had borrowed from the public library again and again. For the first time ever, I owned my own copies of *Emma, Great Expectations, Jane Eyre, and Little Women.* This was thanks to my parents, who kick-started my classics library in my first year in high school.

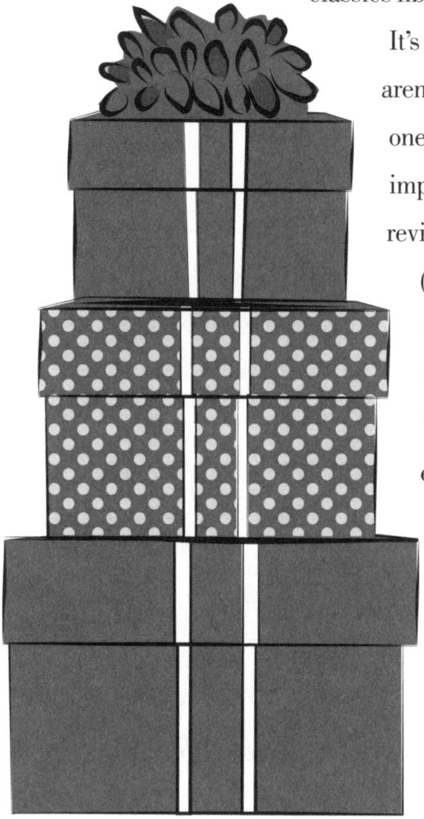

It's funny that the gifts I remember aren't the hot items of the moment everyone else seemed to want. The gifts that impressed me most were the ones I revisited again and again. Because I was (and still am) a theater lover, some Christmases my present was tickets to a musical I really wanted to see in Toronto. Sometimes, due to my parents' budget, the tickets weren't for during the holidays but for a few months later because that meant they could get a good deal. Then when the time came, we would make a day of it in the city.

Experiences not only make great gifts but foster anticipation.

And not only do we get the excitement of opening the promised experience on Christmas morning, but the thoughts behind the gifts stretch beyond *just* Christmas Day.

Christmas shopping can get a bad rap (or wrap, as it were) because of major, panic-inducing crowds and worries about budget and going into the red on our credit cards. But we also want to ensure that our gifts reflect how much we value the recipients. The desire for thoughtful gift-giving shouldn't lead to forgoing presents altogether; it just means we should differentiate gifts of value from *stuff*.

In addition, the stress of Christmas often comes from the burden of pressure we put on ourselves, believing everything, including our gifts, must be *perfect* more than authentic. If made-for-TV Christmas movies show us anything, it's often that the Christmas pageant can lose its conductor an hour before curtain and the town snow festival can be thrown by unseasonable weather. The message is that sometimes makeshift Christmases—and even our less-than-obviously spectacular gifts—are the most memorable.

Taking the stress out of gift-giving might not seem completely feasible, but we can make it more bearable, more affordable, and more fun.

Customized VIEWING LIST

Part of the joy of watching made-for-TV Christmas movies is their colorful palette—the brilliant window and shop displays, the wrapped gifts with accessories and bows presented lovingly by professional set designers who inspire us to try our hand at similar arrangements. Each of the films listed here feature the magic of Christmas shopping. Whether a department store Santa finds true love, or a business tycoon gets in touch with the toy department he once so loved, shopping is less about commercial and monetary gain and more about experience, history, care, and tradition.

Perhaps our budgets don't allow for the splendidly wrapped gifts we see on television. And despite our best efforts, our significant other might not be the recipient of a beautiful piece of jewelry and our kids might not tear at the ribbons and paper to find the latest high-tech gadget. It can be discouraging when we're unable to put what we feel and want for our loved one into a gift that would excite them, but that doesn't mean we should dread shopping for Christmas gifts. Instead, we can set an expectation for gifts that have deep meaning.

Whether we save up for months or cut back on expenses to ensure the perfect gift is procured or we have a family discussion about what truly authentic gifts mean, shopping and gift-giving should be reclaimed as a delight of the holiday season, not a chore.

- *With Love, Christmas:* Unbeknownst to two office rivals,

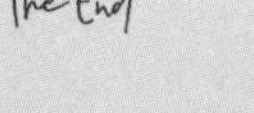
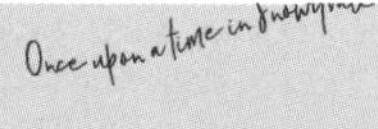

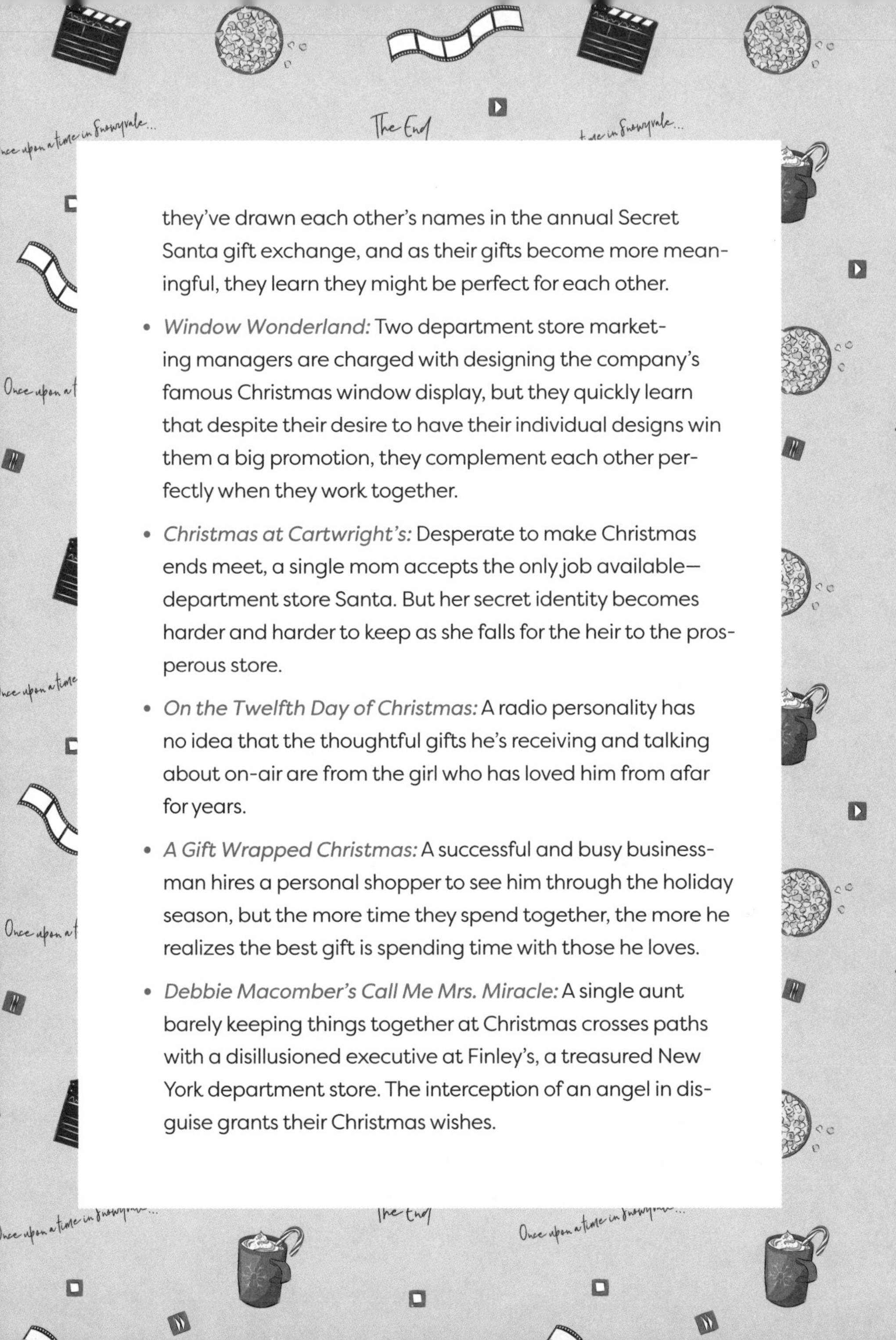

they've drawn each other's names in the annual Secret Santa gift exchange, and as their gifts become more meaningful, they learn they might be perfect for each other.

- *Window Wonderland:* Two department store marketing managers are charged with designing the company's famous Christmas window display, but they quickly learn that despite their desire to have their individual designs win them a big promotion, they complement each other perfectly when they work together.
- *Christmas at Cartwright's:* Desperate to make Christmas ends meet, a single mom accepts the only job available—department store Santa. But her secret identity becomes harder and harder to keep as she falls for the heir to the prosperous store.
- *On the Twelfth Day of Christmas:* A radio personality has no idea that the thoughtful gifts he's receiving and talking about on-air are from the girl who has loved him from afar for years.
- *A Gift Wrapped Christmas:* A successful and busy businessman hires a personal shopper to see him through the holiday season, but the more time they spend together, the more he realizes the best gift is spending time with those he loves.
- *Debbie Macomber's Call Me Mrs. Miracle:* A single aunt barely keeping things together at Christmas crosses paths with a disillusioned executive at Finley's, a treasured New York department store. The interception of an angel in disguise grants their Christmas wishes.

Taking the stress out of gift-giving might not seem completely feasible, but we can make it more bearable, more affordable, and more fun.

Make Christmas Shopping Fun Again

- Avoid whatever makes shopping a stressful activity for you by planning ahead. For instance, keep a box of purchased Christmas gift items you've seen on sale or that just caught your eye throughout the year.
- Rather than stress over what to buy for children, consider this advice for how to buy Christmas gifts for them; I see it online every year: one thing they *want*, one thing they *need*, and one thing to *read*.
- Most online retailers, such as Amazon, have a "save for later" option in a cart. Throughout the year, keep an eye out for items you think would be perfect for a gift recipient or a stocking. Then when Christmas shows up, you already have options in digital storage.
- Wrap presents inside another gift—like a sweatshirt or pair of socks or a reusable tote. This saves spending money on wrapping paper, gift bags, and gift boxes and helps the environment too! Even if you get tangled up in masking tape or fail to fold an item with perfectly creased lines, this is a wonderful and creative way to show you took the time to think uniquely about the outside of the main gift.

Make Christmas Shopping an Event

- If shopping is keeping you from making social plans with friends or family you haven't seen in a while, incorporate it into a shared outing along with a movie or lunch.
- Invite your girlfriends over for a Cyber Monday event, the Monday after the U.S. Thanksgiving Day. Compare online prices, flip your laptop screens around to show your friends the cutest socks and most festive pj's you find, and make everyone's to-do list more bearable with some in-person brainstorming for what to purchase for the hard-to-buy-for people on their lists.
- Go window-shopping, even if you can't afford to buy anything at the ritzy stores. Many department stores reveal their big Christmas displays after the Santa Claus parade or tree lighting. If you don't live in an urban center, make a day trip to one nearby.
- Hit church bazaars, charity events, and local Christmas markets. You can't go wrong with homemade crafts, and a fun, out-of-the-box day with family and friends can make for a great experience. Specifically look for the festivals, fairs, and markets hosted by different cultures in your community. They provide an opportunity to learn about Christmas traditions in a different way, and you may find some unique gifts. Follow your

town or city's municipal or tourist accounts on social media to keep an eye out for these.

- Instead of having a girlfriends' gift exchange before Christmas, when items are most often at their full and highest price, have one the week of New Year's. This takes advantage of post-Christmas sales and clearances.

Be a Savvy Secret Santa

- A donation to a food bank or local charity in a coworker's name is a great idea if you're stuck on what to gift that person in a Christmas exchange.
- World Vision International and ChildFund International (formerly Christian Children's Fund) offer the opportunity to donate for the purchase of livestock—like a goat, a cow, or even a duck—to benefit children in developing nations.
- Think beyond your coworkers to their lives. Is someone always talking about his kids? Is her cubicle full of photos of her beloved cat? Use some of your allotted budget to buy a small gift for the other people or the pets they love. This shows you're willing to invest in their personal lives as well as in your working relationship.

Create the Perfect Christmas Stocking

- Think of the stocking as an appetizer to another gift. If you're buying a set of clothing, put a matching accessory into the stocking as a precursor to the main gift.
- Think of the stocking as an accent for another gift. If you've purchased a new electronic, put an extra adapter or charger in the stocking.
- Make one stocking gift a small pencil box, makeup case, or jewelry holder and place smaller gifts inside.
- Oranges, apples, nuts, and wrapped chocolates and other candies are classic additions to any stocking.
- A great way to encourage social interaction, especially for teens who tend to hide at home during the holiday break, is giving a gift card to a coffee shop or restaurant with a note encouraging the recipient to take along a friend or coworker.

Make Christmas Shopping Special: Pay It Forward

- If you're about to place a Christmas-related order online but are just shy of the free-shipping minimum, text a sister or friend to see if you can include an order for her. That not only allows her to check off a holiday purchase but neither of you pays for shipping.
- If you're going shopping at a wholesale store and your friend or neighbor doesn't have a membership, offer to take their Christmas list too.
- If you're breaking up a long shopping trip with a stop at a favorite coffee shop, grab a hot chocolate for the volunteer manning a charity kettle nearby.

Start a New TRADITION

Does your office Christmas party, small group, or book club Secret Santa exchange make you feel financial pressure or stress? Or would you like to swap out the White Elephant or Yankee Swap for an exchange more lasting and meaningful? The world is full of people with hidden hobbies and talents. Perhaps you can find a way to ensure Christmas traditions will allow you to get to know your coworkers a little better.

If you're used to shopping online, try an easy "pay it forward" by visiting local, independently owned shops and securing the same merchandise there. A trick is to go early enough in the season so even if your neighborhood store doesn't carry what you want, you'll still have time to order it online for a before-Christmas delivery.

Festive FACTS

Miracle on 34th Street is a classic film that examines the magic of belief in Santa Claus amid the bustle of Christmas. It also recalls the wonder of a response to a letter to the editor published in the *New York Sun* near the turn of the twentieth century.

In September 1897, Francis Pharcellus Church, a hardened, Civil War veteran editor, penned that response to a coroner's young daughter, Virginia O'Hanlon, who wanted to confirm the existence of Santa Claus. Now the most reprinted editorial letter in the English language, Church's address, including the line "Yes, Virginia, there is a Santa Claus," has captured the hearts and imaginations of generations.

Along with Christmas shopping comes the almost inevitable appearance of a mall or department store Santa. No matter your belief or traditions, recognizing the goodwill that passed between Church and an eight-year-old girl can capture your heart too.

The Book Lover's Christmas

I once saw you sell a book to a single mother for a penny. That will be your annual lease a year now. One penny.

KAREN KINGSBURY'S *THE BRIDGE*

Part of my cultural heritage has lately become a popular and constantly shared internet meme. My Icelandic ancestors had a book lover's dream Christmas tradition that included gifting family and friends the written word. *Jólabókaflóð*, Icelandic for "Yule Book Flood," originated in the years around the Second World War when foreign imports were restricted but paper was cheap. Since then, every Christmas Eve, Icelandic families exchange books and sweets and spend the best hours of the yuletide reading.

As I am a voracious bookworm, the Christmas holidays are a time for me to revisit favorite Christmas-set stories as well as use the break to catch up on my reading list. Since I was ten, I have had a tradition of reading *Vienna Prelude* by Bodie Thoene every year at Christmas. Though the book, a historical romance set in Austria, isn't technically a Christmas novel, many of the scenes most integral to the story take place at Christmastime.

Something about returning to our favorite stories again and again is comforting, and Christmas reading is a tradition I think should be cultivated as often as possible, whether that means displaying holiday-themed novels and short stories around the tree to be perused by guests and family or ensuring that favorite books are gifted every year.

Stories have a way of binding people together as well as contributing to the narrative of memory. Is anything more fulfilling than sitting around the dinner table and recalling Christmases past? Shedding a few tears, certainly, but also bending over with laughter? Stories are a gift. Everyone knows the one person in the family who tells a specific anecdote exactly the right way. Introducing books is another way of continuing an important tradition of community. Books are also a great unifier, and Christmas is the best time to find that commonality with family and friends. To give a book is to give the first sentence of a prospective conversation. Gifting beloved books invites others to peek through a window to your world. If you love a book's universe and opinions and share that treasure with another, the conversation has already started.

Create the Perfect Bookish Atmosphere

Whether cuddling up for some solo reading time or hosting a holiday book club, you want to ensure that your guests feel perfectly comfortable, cozy and immersed in the holiday spirit. Here are some ideas:

- Simmer orange peels with a half teaspoon of cinnamon on medium heat to fill your house with a festive aroma.
- Ask your local florist or Christmas tree farm for leftover pine branches or boughs for a piney scent in your home.
- Have cookies baking as your guests arrive so the house smells of fresh goodies (that you can all consume later).
- Open a nearby window a smidgeon for just enough wintry air.
- Mull cider in a slow cooker to keep its warm aroma and tasty goodness near at hand.
- For cozy book discussions, keep the lighting low. Candlelight, Christmas tree lights, and garland lights all create immediate atmosphere.

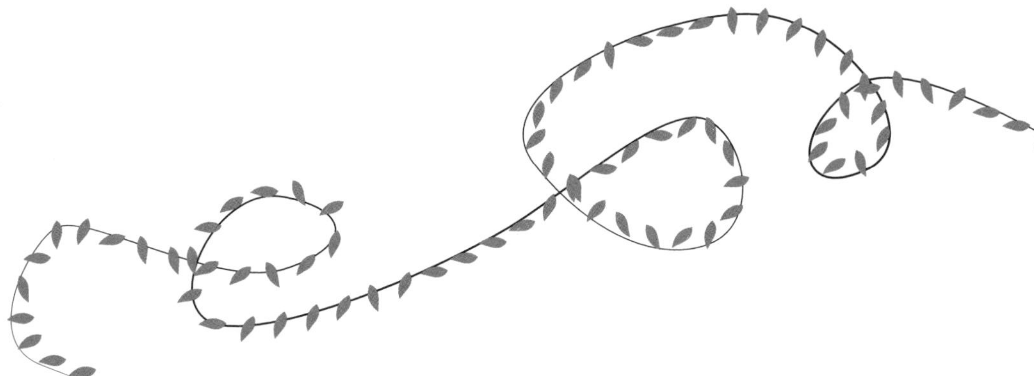

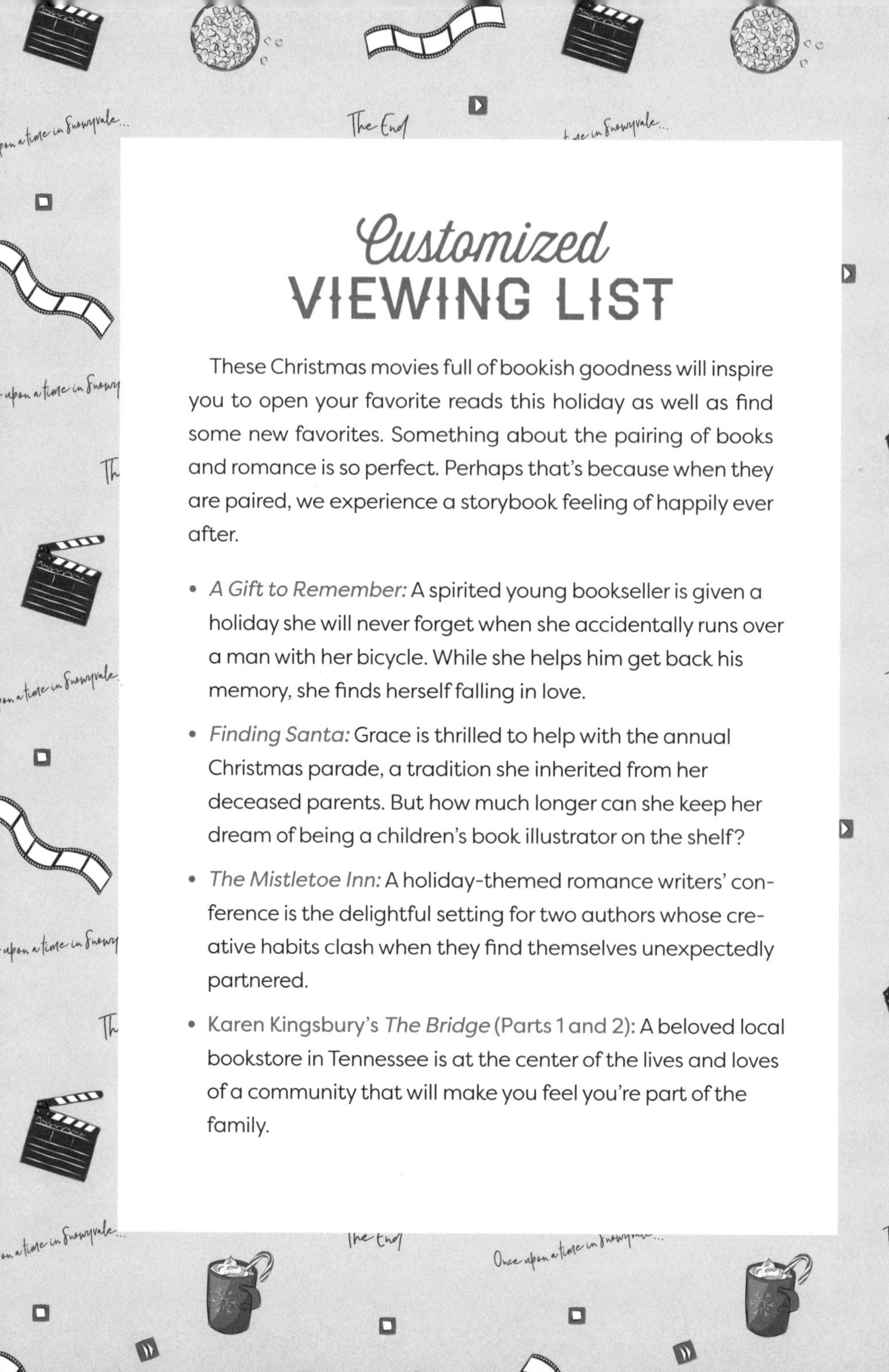

Customized VIEWING LIST

These Christmas movies full of bookish goodness will inspire you to open your favorite reads this holiday as well as find some new favorites. Something about the pairing of books and romance is so perfect. Perhaps that's because when they are paired, we experience a storybook feeling of happily ever after.

- *A Gift to Remember:* A spirited young bookseller is given a holiday she will never forget when she accidentally runs over a man with her bicycle. While she helps him get back his memory, she finds herself falling in love.
- *Finding Santa:* Grace is thrilled to help with the annual Christmas parade, a tradition she inherited from her deceased parents. But how much longer can she keep her dream of being a children's book illustrator on the shelf?
- *The Mistletoe Inn:* A holiday-themed romance writers' conference is the delightful setting for two authors whose creative habits clash when they find themselves unexpectedly partnered.
- Karen Kingsbury's *The Bridge* (Parts 1 and 2): A beloved local bookstore in Tennessee is at the center of the lives and loves of a community that will make you feel you're part of the family.

- *A Joyous Christmas:* A popular self-help author and speaker finds herself questioning the advice she's giving when a small-town experience and a long-held secret inspire her to look deep inside her heart.
- *Christmas Around the Corner:* A high-powered New York venture capitalist visits a charming small town to loan her business expertise to its small shops and finds romance and a deep love for a neighborhood bookstore in the process.

- Light a fire in your fireplace. If you don't have a fireplace, consider using an electric space heater that emulates the look of a fireplace. Or insert a DVD simulating a fire in a fireplace for display on your TV screen. You can even run a YouTube video of a roaring fire on your computer screen while your guests arrive.
- Providing fuzzy Christmas socks or slippers makes wonderful party favors for your guests, and they'll keep them comfy throughout your gathering too.
- Spritz your comfiest throws, blankets, sweaters, and scarves with pine air freshener and arrange them in a basket for your guests to use throughout your time together.
- Create festive bookplates for your guests by buying plain ones and then applying seasonal stickers or stenciling. (You can also affix them to books you give as gifts.)

Your Made-for-TV-Movie-Loving Christmas Reading List

Some of the best-beloved made-for-TV Christmas movies are based on books, while others make you feel as if you're watching holiday magic unfold on screen with the power of your imagination.

Here are highly recommended festive reads adapted for the small screen.

- The Mrs. Miracle series—Debbie Macomber
- *The Christmas Secret*—Donna VanLiere
- *Miss Christmas*—Gigi Garrett
- *The Bridge*—Karen Kingsbury
- The Father Christmas trilogy—Robin Jones Gunn
- *Christmas Eve at Friday Harbor* (adapted as *Christmas with Holly*)—Lisa Kleypas
- *The Goodbye Bride* (adapted as *Christmas on My Mind*)—Denise Hunter

Here are highly recommended festive holiday books that read like a movie:

- *A Cliché Christmas*—Nicole Deese
- *One Enchanted Eve*—Melissa Tagg
- *Starring Christmas*—Allison Pittman and Rachel McMillan
- *The Perfect Love Song*—Patti Callahan Henry
- *Christmas at Harrington's*—Melody Carlson
- *The Wedding Dress Christmas*—Rachel Hauck

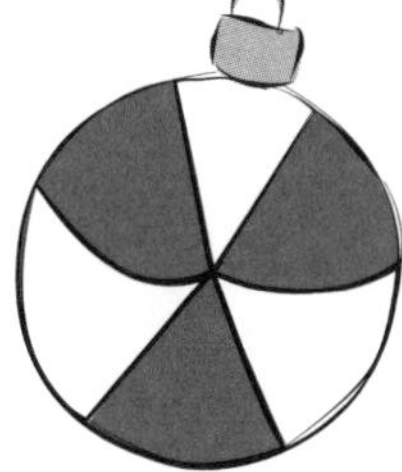

Start a New TRADITION

Instill the gift of the written word in someone with the gift of experience. Take a loved one or friend book shopping, grabbing a favorite hot drink while there if you can. Either through the promise of a book purchase or with prepaid gift certificates in tow, a shared love of reading is a gift to revisit every year.

Festive FACTS

As well as Dickens's *A Christmas Carol*, Clement Clarke Moore's *The Night Before Christmas* is the source of many of the Christmas emblems and traditions we embrace to this day. Initially penned as *A Visit from St. Nicholas*, this work is not only America's most-often quoted poem but a tree-side staple of many American traditions. Generally believed to have been composed by Moore on a snowy winter's day during a sleigh-drawn shopping trip, the St. Nicholas of the piece is based on the Dutch *Sinterklaas*. The traditions of hanging stockings by the chimney and the idea of airborne reindeer pulling Santa's sleigh on his many Christmas Eve errands gained their popularity from the verses of this long ballad.

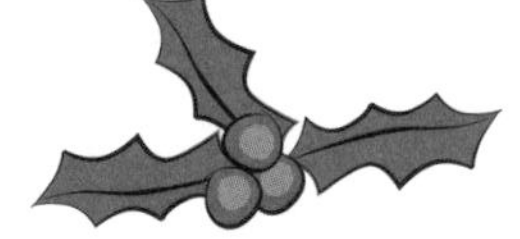

Carols
Carols

The Music Lover's Christmas

He told me all of these people carry Christmas in their heart, and I should think of the audience as one big family. And I think of that to this day every time I have stage fright.

OUR CHRISTMAS LOVE SONG

The link between music and memory is so strong that it's easy to see why Christmas music is so popular. Even the happiest holiday songs can seem melancholy when the nostalgic bug bites and we think of loved ones now gone and Christmases past. Christmas music is also a testament to the human power of memory. Most of us hear these traditional hits for only a few weeks out of the year, yet we remember the melodies and lyrics a year later.

I know of one reason these songs set themselves so deeply in hearts and minds. For religious people, Christmas music relays the power of the message integral to our celebration. And imparted in the words sung by pop stars and blasted across department store aisles once a year, that message so deeply meaningful is spread to so many.

Without a doubt, my favorite part of Christmas is the music.

Listening to songs written hundreds of years ago, performed by some of the most beautiful voices of the modern world, takes me back home to my parents' living room, sitting by the tree while our favorite albums provide a lovely backdrop. Christmas music is so ingrained in my memory that I don't recall a time when I didn't know the words to every last song on the Carpenters' Christmas album my dad played over and over again and on the well-loved cassettes with music produced by Michael W. Smith and Amy Grant.

Music is an incredible gift. It brings people together in collective memory as we hum and recall the lyrics together, but it also acts as a canvas for the words spoken over it as we engage in conversations and make new memories that will last a lifetime. Whether holding a candle at a Christmas Eve service in a hallowed church where the organ chords rise to the rafters, caroling off-key for a local food bank, or merely singing along with Mariah Carey on our iTunes playlist on the subway train, the music of Christmas tells a story and anchors us to Christmases that have come before and the promise of Christmases that will come. I can think of no other time of the year that elicits such a vast musical response—for those who believe in the religious tenets of Christmas and those who simply enjoy a good melody alike.

Caroling 101

- Check for local carol sings in your neighborhood. Start with church websites.
- Take your love for caroling somewhere it matters. Retirement communities, hospices, and hospitals are wonderful places to spread holiday cheer. Email the administrators in the fall to determine when and where your caroling might be well received. (A tip: Because Christmas is not a universally celebrated holiday and being mindful of other traditions, prepare a range of generic, inclusive songs every listener will find accessible and enjoy.)
- If friends and family aren't usually churchgoers like you, Christmas is the perfect time to invite them to accompany you to a traditional Sunday service where you can all sing your heart out to carols.
- Remember that though caroling is a somewhat archaic tradition, at heart most people love Christmas music and the Christmas spirit. Don't be afraid to let go and make an idiot of yourself! Sometimes it's fun to allow others to see you "let down your hair."

Customized
VIEWING LIST

Each of the movies listed here is designed to appeal to the music lover, and I believe a music lover is in all of us. From a composer working at an instrument store to the enchantment of a ballet honoring Tchaikovsky's masterpiece, from Elvis's famed home in Memphis to the legend of Dolly Parton in Tennessee, the makers of Christmas movies are aware of the delicious effect music has on their viewers. Many Christmas films ensure that their soundtracks are upbeat as well as nostalgic, coloring moments of romance and memory in the characters' lives with songs treasured by many.

- *Angels and Ornaments:* A mysterious composition from the Second World War creates a bond between two music-shop employees in a movie that celebrates carols.
- *A Song for Christmas:* A pop star is stranded in a small town for Christmas and not only finds a path through her writer's block but the opportunity for a family Christmas she's never had.
- *Christmas at Graceland:* Elvis Presley's famous home is a supporting character in the story of a single mom who brings her kids to Graceland for Christmas and reconnects with a talented country singer she once loved.

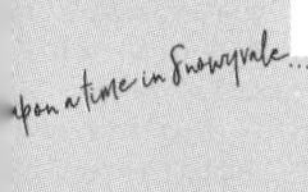

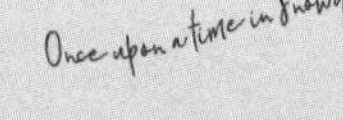

- *A Christmas Melody:* A single mom finds unexpected love when her daughter has the opportunity to sing a solo in the school Christmas concert. This film costars pop star Mariah Carey.
- *Our Christmas Love Song:* Melody's performance at the Grand Ole Opry is a smash—until a rival country star claims that the holiday song she performs is plagiarized. The looming lawsuit drives her home and back to her long-lost sweetheart.
- *Christmas at Dollywood:* Dolly Parton makes a cameo in this story about a single mom who returns to her hometown to produce an event at the legendary Dollywood. When she meets the park's entertainment director, they clash on many fronts—but not on love.

Create the Perfect Christmas Playlist

Whether hosting a party or chaperoning a shopping trip that requires some festive tunes in the car, a playlist can enhance the Christmas mood.

- *Consider all listeners.* Ensure a variety of tempos and genres to appeal to every holiday lover.
- *Include nostalgic favorites and new classics.* Introduce listeners to new favorite songs that might be classics in a few years.
- *Every song tells a story.* Open your past and heart to listeners by letting them in on the emotional connection you have to a song.
- *Contrast wistful and melancholy ballads with upbeat and happy numbers.* While some mournful chords conjure the solemnity and reflective mood of the season, a counterbalance of these tempos with upbeat pieces will endear you to your guests.
- *Step outside your comfort zone.* Google the most recent Christmas hits and use the prompts from sites like Spotify and iTunes to broaden your musical horizons.

The "Silent Night" Chapel

For many, Salzburg, Austria, is synonymous with music. Once home of the famed Wolfgang Amadeus Mozart and later to the Hollywood movie featuring the von Trapp family—***The Sound of Music***—its hills are filled with notes and song. Perhaps most importantly, it's the birthplace of arguably the most *popular* Christmas carol ever penned—"Silent Night." If you can't make a pilgrimage to this iconic site, then visit the amazing 360-degree provided at stillenacht.com for an immersive experience of both the interior and exterior of the chapel.

"Silent Night" should be treated like porcelain. So long ago was it forged, and so precariously, that its fragility through the hunger and uncertainty of the Napoleonic Wars was fortified by the legend that saw its journey beyond its Alp-side home and into our culture. In fact, "Silent Night" and its humble origins from a small Austrian village can inspire us to meditate more on the holiday songs we hear and can sing in a state of immediate remembrance, mouthing words we've impressed to memory even if we don't linger on their meaning.

Start a New TRADITION

Check your local newspaper listings and your streaming services for holiday concerts. From Washington, D.C.'s Christmas tree ceremony to the Vienna Boys' Choir and even Westminster Abbey, you have options for watching a Christmas concert with your family. For example, every New Year's Eve, PBS broadcasts the New Year's Eve Concert from the Golden Hall of the Musikverein in Vienna. A classical and historical concert featuring a range of masterpieces, including Strauss, the concert is a wonderful introduction to a beautiful world.

Festive FACTS

Some of the most beautiful and beloved carols have come out of times of conflict and war. Just as "Silent Night" came out of a dark and hungry time for Austrians under the threat of Napoleon, so several glorious songs of hope and the promise of the nativity resulted from the American Civil War. "O Little Town of Bethlehem," "It Came Upon a Midnight Clear," and "I Heard the Bells on Christmas Day" are all examples of songs that came out of the War Between the States.

In World War I, as several young men spent Christmas across the barren trenches surrounding an area called No Man's Land, an unprecedented Christmas truce found them lowering their rifles in a gesture of solidarity and seasonal recognition. Christmas 1914 was a bleak and violent one until the dawn of Christmas Day, when German soldiers rose at dawn calling out "Merry Christmas" in the native tongue of their enemy. Unarmed, they assured the allies that they approached in peace and goodwill. Throughout the day, trees were crudely decorated, greetings and songs filled the heavy air, and a game of football blurred the lines between the enemies.

The Royal Christmas

Once upon a time, in a land called Buffalo, there lived a little girl who dreamt of traveling to faraway places where the people sang for a lark and danced on a whim, where houses were filled with calliopes and music boxes, mechanical dolls and cuckoo clocks.

A PRINCESS FOR CHRISTMAS

Everyone wants a royal happily ever after. Few experiences spark the imagination like watching Prince Harry wed Meghan Markle or Prince William walk Kate Middleton through Westminster Abbey as she wore a stunning dress. Most little girls imagine themselves princesses and visit the same fairy tales over and over again. What better time to dream of a fairy tale than at Christmas, when we not only believe in flying reindeer but wish upon stars, hoping our dreams will come true? As well, our fascination with royalty might have to do with their history and tradition, which are as magnificent as the titles and customs of lords and ladies.

Not everyone has the opportunity to hop over to London to skate at Somerset House on the Strand or visit the crown jewels in the

Tower of London, with Christmas lights displayed from Oxford Street to Piccadilly Circus. But that doesn't mean you can't host a royal-themed tea for your friends and family as the perfect backdrop for a Christmas movie. Whether you find some Christmas crackers or a few costume-jewelry tiaras or pull out your grandmother's heirloom tea service (or the mismatched pieces you found at Goodwill), incorporating some of the genteel and time-honored traditions of the royals can enhance your Christmas experience and make for a fun themed event. So send out invitations *by royal decree* and plan a holiday-themed high tea.

Hold a Christmas-Royal-Movie-Viewing Tea

- Bring out lace doilies and your fanciest real or fake china.
- Check out church bazaars for serving platters or even a tea tray. Many are held in November just before the Christmas rush.
- Serve traditional high tea sandwiches cut crustless and finger length and served with a parsley garnish. They might feature your favorite egg salad or salmon recipe, chicken salad spread, or the traditional cucumber sandwich easily created with thin, almost transparent cucumber slices and cream cheese on white bread.
- Make or buy petits fours for your lovely tea tray.
- Decorate your sugar bowl by adding some green and red sprinkles.

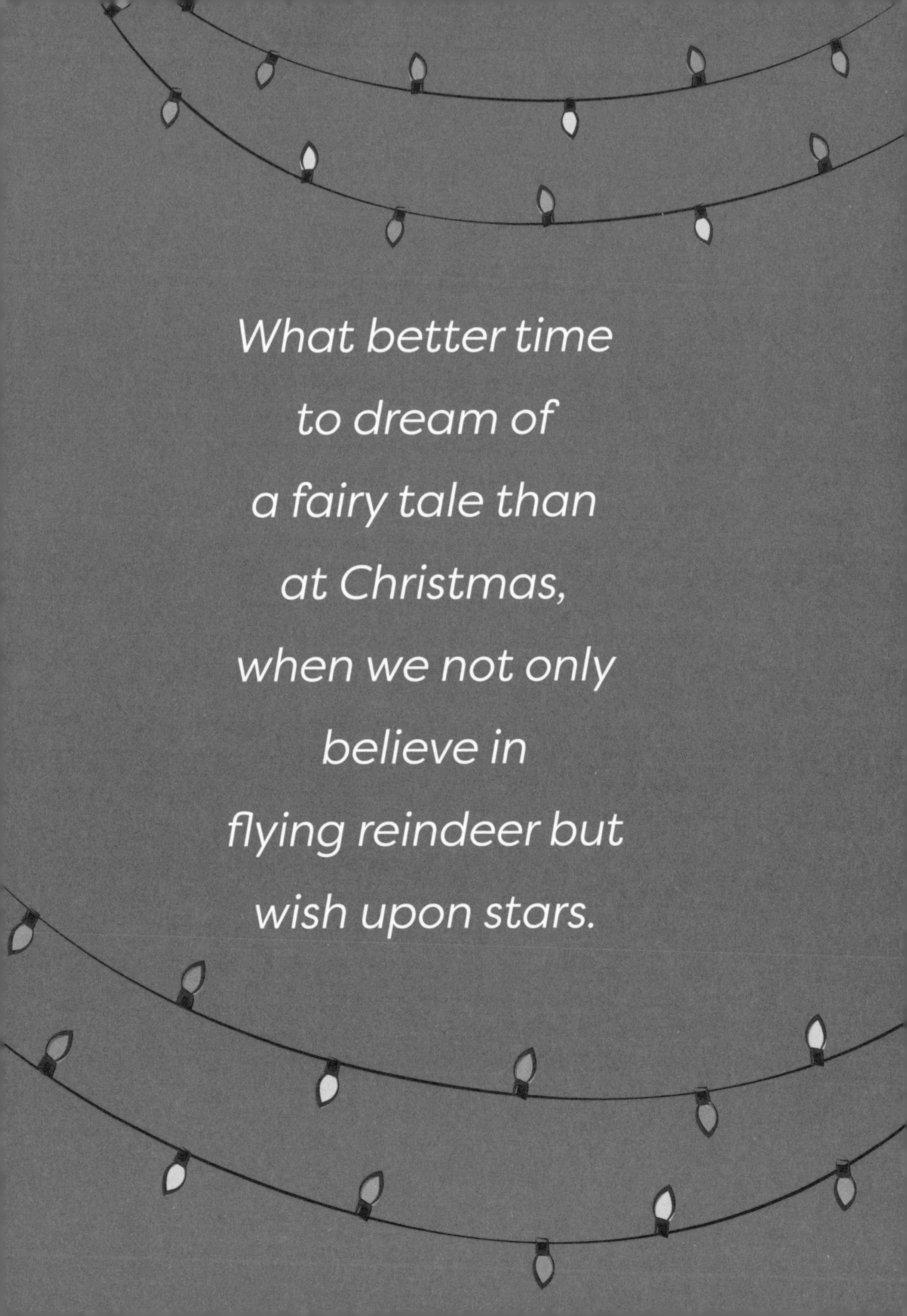

What better time

to dream of

a fairy tale than

at Christmas,

when we not only

believe in

flying reindeer but

wish upon stars.

Customized VIEWING LIST

Regardless of the season, royal love stories are always on the docket. Will the princess find true love with a visiting businessman? Will the prince find that his daughter's tutor stirs his heart? For those who love grand ballrooms and castles that recall the age of chivalry and derring-do, several royal-themed movie romances can melt your heart. From a princess disguising herself as a commoner to escape the pressures of royal life during a visit to New York City to a seamstress who finds herself gracing the royal court (and facing the prince's exacting mother), these are movies that appeal to the dreamer in all of us. And those royal settings are offered at Christmas as well.

- *A Christmas Prince:* A young reporter is promised a big career move if she travels to a European castle and digs up the truth about a prince's impending nuptials. Then she finds herself falling for him.
- *A Royal Christmas:* The heir to the throne falls for a seamstress while completing his education in America. Complications ensue when he takes this commoner home as his holiday guest.
- *Once Upon a Holiday:* A princess visiting New York during Christmas goes rogue when she takes a day away from her royal duties, then falls for a charming home renovator in the process.

- *Crown for Christmas:* A maid recently on the unemployment line finds the chance of a lifetime as a governess for a young princess. But when she finds herself falling for the girl's royal single father, she gets more than she bargained for and a crash course in royal etiquette.
- *A Christmas in Royal Fashion:* A handsome prince believes an American fashion show can help him bring a growing industry back to his small kingdom, but he doesn't expect to fall in love with a charming young assistant in the process.

- Include a bouquet of cinnamon sticks as part of your decor for added ambience and a Christmassy scent.
- Ask your local bakery if they offer dyed red-and-green bread during the holiday season. If they do, buy some!
- Give your guests titles (Lady, Duchess, Your Highness, Princess) and feature place cards with them at their spots.

Make Christmas Petits Fours

In a pinch, store-bought truffles, decorated lemon squares, or brownies can easily represent the dainty offerings of a formal tea spread.

Petits Fours

2 eggs
2 egg yolks
1 cup sugar
2 cups all-purpose flour
2 tsp. baking powder
½ cup milk
5 T. butter, melted

Glaze

4 cups sugar
2 cups water
¼ tsp. cream of tartar
3 cups powdered sugar
1 tube each red and green decorating frosting
Holiday sprinkles

Preheat oven to 350°.

In a large bowl, beat the eggs and egg yolks until they're slightly thickened. Gradually add the sugar, beating until the mixture is thick and lemon colored. In a medium bowl, combine the flour and baking powder and then gradually add that to the egg mixture, alternating with the milk and butter, beating well after each addition. (The batter will be thick.)

Spread the batter evenly in a greased-and-floured 15 x 10-inch baking pan. Bake at 350° for 12 to 15 minutes or until a toothpick inserted near the center comes out clean. Cool for 10 minutes before inverting onto a wire rack to cool completely.

Cut a thin slice off each side of the cake before cutting the cake into 1¼-inch squares. Freeze.

In a large saucepan, combine the sugar, water, and cream of tartar. Bring to a boil, without stirring, until a candy thermometer reads 226°. Cool to 100° and then beat in powdered sugar until smooth. Keeping the glaze warm, dip the cake squares into the glaze with a fork, allowing the excess to drip off. Place on wire racks over waxed paper. Add hot water, 1 teaspoon at a time, if the glaze becomes too thick. Let dry completely. Decorate with frosting and sprinkles.

Yields 70 petits fours

Some of the genteel and time-honored traditions of the royals can enhance your Christmas experience and make for a fun themed event.

Royal Etiquette Checklist

- Hold your teacup properly. Use your thumb and index finger to hold the top of the handle while your middle finger supports the bottom of the cup.
- Sip your tea from the same spot on the rim so you don't leave lipstick stains all across the cup.
- Serve the tea from a pot, not with individual tea bags.
- Don't cross your legs but rather your ankles to "sit like a lady."
- Subtle or pale-pink nail polish is the only color permissible for the royal family.
- Nude panty hose must be worn at all times.
- Hats are a must at afternoon gatherings.
- When the Queen finishes eating, everyone is finished, no matter what part of the meal it is.

Start a New TRADITION

Christmas crackers (not the edible kind) are a staple of Christmas traditions in the United Kingdom, and they're also widely available in North America. Each cracker is festively decorated and has a toy or treat inside. You can make your own or buy them online or at your favorite department store.

In the United Kingdom, the Royal Family's Christmas traditions have been held for centuries. Even as far back as King Henry VIII, Christmas traditions and songs were a mainstay of the court during the holiday season. In fact, King Henry himself wrote a Christmas carol, "Green Groweth the Holly," which many believe was his own take on the popular tune "The Holly and the Ivy."

In more recent times, the Royal Family has held and still holds Christmas traditions, such as the annual Queen's Speech from Buckingham Palace. Every December 25, the BBC airs a recorded message from the Queen that offers her greetings to her subjects not only in Britain but in her colonies, such as Australia and Canada.

The Classic Christmas

Each man's life touches so many other lives. When he isn't around he leaves an awful hole, doesn't he?

IT'S A WONDERFUL LIFE

Something about Christmas often makes us want to polish our Mary Jane shoes and straighten our collars. We want to buy a new dress for the company party and slick our hair straight when we descend the staircase to the tree and presents on Christmas morning. Because it's such a special occasion, we want to treat it with the reverence it deserves. The season allows us to bring out the formal dress we bought on clearance, apply the perfect makeup, and don the unique, painful-on-our-heels-but-perfect shoes. Christmas is classy. And Christmas is classic.

In a culture of smartphones that seem to need an upgrade every five minutes and streaming services that require some kind of degree to decode, we enjoy a throwback to the classics. The fashion meets us again and again, and period-set dramas are all the rage when it comes to viewership numbers. With Christmas nostalgia comes a longing for the past, sure, but not just *our* past but also a different point in history. It seems that the more chaos that erupts in the world, the more desperate we are to cling to what we view as a more innocent time. Christmases of yesteryear are featured in commercials and advertisements and relived in classic black-and-white films such as ***Miracle on 34th Street*** and ***It's a Wonderful Life***. The chimes of the latest gadget and the ability to command a Siri robot or Alexa device is a far cry from Currier and Ives, but at its core, the classic tenets of Christmas—peace, goodwill, sharing, and kindness—are the hallmarks of the season.

Christmas Letter Writing

- Host a formal letter-writing party with your friends. Encourage them to bring the names of one or two people they would like to write to.
- Send paper invites to your friends and family and have everyone dress to a theme. Perhaps a black-and-white Christmas, or "Holly and Ivy." Encourage your friends to think about correspondence as it was back in the day, a daily, honored event.

- Provide stamps and fancy pens and stationery as well as either a stamp seal or stickers to help add to the glamour of the letters.
- Display printed-out examples of classic love letters. (Hint: A quick internet search for World War I love letters; those written from Napoleon to his wife, Josephine; and from John Adams to his wife, Abigail, is one way to capture classic examples.)
- An internet search for examples of calligraphy can provide your guests with ideas for how to add flourish to their letters with a little something extra.

Christmas Card Hacks

If you're anything like me, you have the best intentions to send Christmas cards to friends and family near and far, but you often leave it to the last minute and don't make it. Have everything ready before the Christmas rush keeps you from getting the cards in the mail.

- Stock up on Christmas cards directly after New Year's Day when you can get a hefty discount (and don't forget you bought them when Christmas approaches again).
- If you're sending out a family Christmas card

At its core,

the classic tenets

of Christmas—

peace, goodwill,

sharing,

and kindness—

are the hallmarks

of the season.

complete with a photo, don't necessarily have a special Christmas-themed photo taken. Use one from a fun vacation or event in the last few months. Sure, you might be in shorts and not a Santa hat, but the Christmas card can act as a recollection of the year, and those who love you most are going to do so year-round anyway. It's a terrific way to share a memory as the old year closes. With this in mind, you can have a printer prepare the cards or photos in the fall so they'll be ready for mailing in early December.

- Keep your address book updated throughout the year so you aren't scrambling to find where that recently moved aunt or cousin now gets mail.
- If you know you're going to run into a coworker or friend, plan to give them their Christmas card in person. That will check one person off your list.
- Some late, rainy autumn day, get everything organized. Then address envelopes and affix stamps so when the lights of the Christmas tree are on and you're in the mood to write with a cup of cider at your side, all you have to do is pen your greetings.

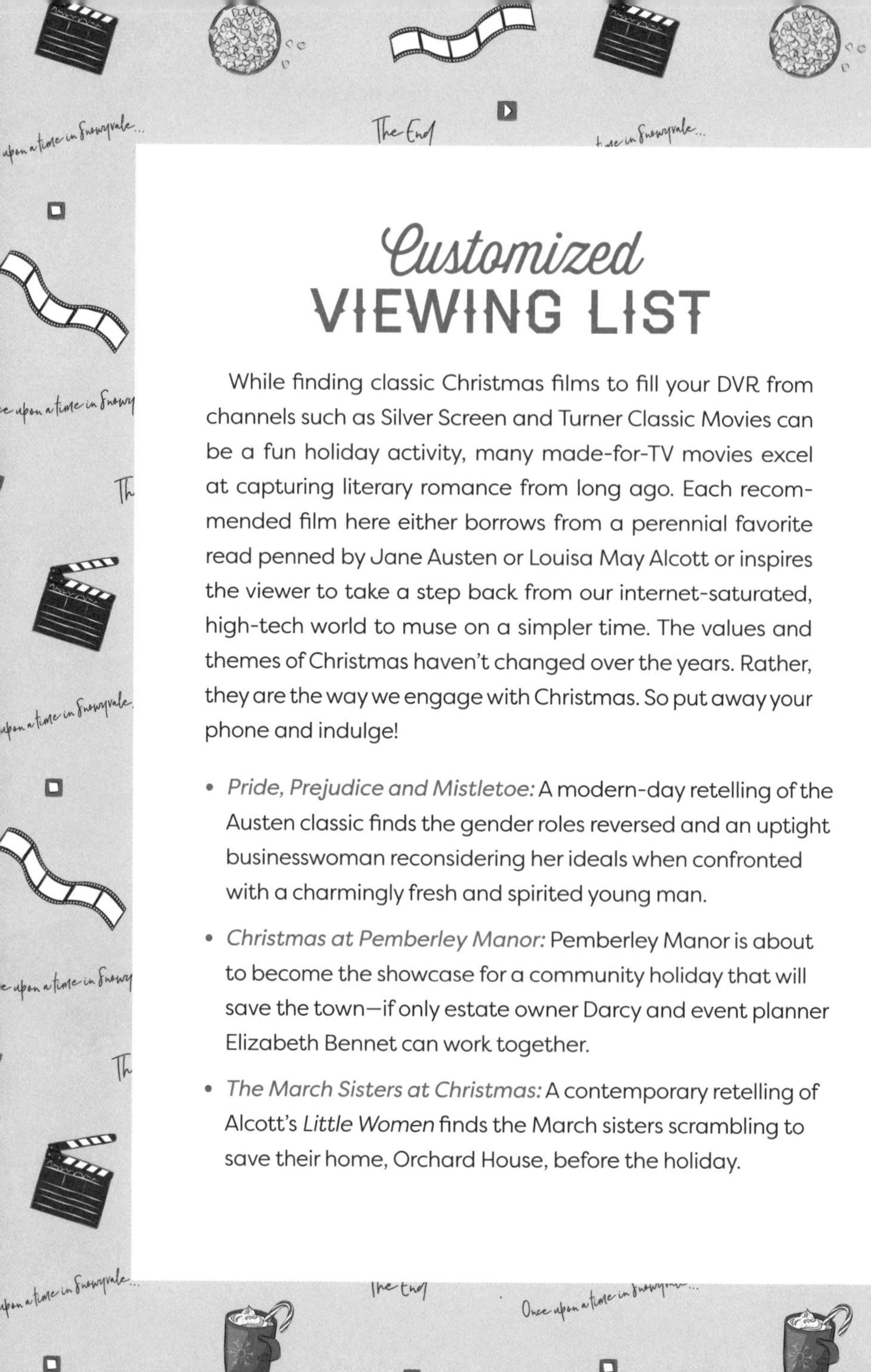

Customized VIEWING LIST

While finding classic Christmas films to fill your DVR from channels such as Silver Screen and Turner Classic Movies can be a fun holiday activity, many made-for-TV movies excel at capturing literary romance from long ago. Each recommended film here either borrows from a perennial favorite read penned by Jane Austen or Louisa May Alcott or inspires the viewer to take a step back from our internet-saturated, high-tech world to muse on a simpler time. The values and themes of Christmas haven't changed over the years. Rather, they are the way we engage with Christmas. So put away your phone and indulge!

- *Pride, Prejudice and Mistletoe:* A modern-day retelling of the Austen classic finds the gender roles reversed and an uptight businesswoman reconsidering her ideals when confronted with a charmingly fresh and spirited young man.
- *Christmas at Pemberley Manor:* Pemberley Manor is about to become the showcase for a community holiday that will save the town—if only estate owner Darcy and event planner Elizabeth Bennet can work together.
- *The March Sisters at Christmas:* A contemporary retelling of Alcott's *Little Women* finds the March sisters scrambling to save their home, Orchard House, before the holiday.

- *The Christmas Train:* Strangers stranded by a derailed Amtrak train find new loves and reconnect with old friends in a story with timeless themes.
- *Signed, Sealed, Delivered for Christmas:* Featuring a quirky and loveable team of employees charged with returning misdirected letters to their owners, the Dead Letter Office at the U.S. Postal Service finds hope with vintage tradition, old-fashioned customs, and a lot of faith.
- *Sense, Sensibility & Snowmen:* A modern romantic comedy with an Austen twist, the party-planning Dashwood sisters meet a challenge when the venue for their party is double-booked and they need to get creative, all while falling for two dashing men.
- *Christmas at the Plaza:* A historian and a Christmas-loving tree decorator visit the past when they take an archival trip into the famous hotel's Christmas traditions of yore.

Forgotten Classic Christmas Specials

Sure, we have our favorite holiday romantic movies and, of course, the annual live TV special the night the tree at Rockefeller Center is lit in New York City. But since the 1950s, when televisions began showing up in every home, Christmas specials—most often of the musical variety—found everyone gathering in the living room (perhaps even eating TV dinners on trays to boot!).

Bob Hope and Bing Crosby had several Christmas TV programs each, but the YouTube and DVD recording sleuth in your household can also go on a treasure hunt for the following specials:

- *A Chipmunk Christmas*
- *The Berenstain Bears' Christmas Tree*
- *The Star Wars Holiday Special*
- *Perry Como's Christmas in New York*
- *The Judy Garland Christmas Show*
- *The Carpenters at Christmas*
- *Dean Martin's California Christmas*

Your Classic Christmas on Social Media

Pinterest and Instagram are two fantastic sites to glean ideas for how to make your Christmas as classic as possible. Creating a collage of what you would like to do for the present holiday or for future Christmases is easy to keep track of online. But Christmas might be more fun if you contributed your own presence to your favorite sites.

Create a hashtag for your friends and family and perhaps even include #ClassicChristmas when you post. Or create a handle for an open Instagram or Pinterest account people can contribute to.

Make the holidays as dapper as possible by dressing up in vintage or classic looks and snapping pics near the town hall Christmas tree or in a favorite deco-style hotel foyer or building decorated for the season.

Make a Vintage Holiday Playlist

Whether recorded decades ago or by a contemporary artist with a classic flair, make sure these favorites are on your playlist:

- Ella Fitzgerald, "What Are You Doing New Year's Eve?"
- Bing Crosby, "Do You Hear What I Hear?"
- Michael Bublé, "Blue Christmas"
- Judy Garland, "Have Yourself a Merry Little Christmas"
- Nat King Cole, "The Christmas Song"
- Doris Day, "Silver Bells"
- The Carpenters, "The Christmas Waltz"
- Andy Williams, "Happy Holidays"
- Josh Groban, "Silent Night"
- The Andrews Sisters, "Sleigh Ride"

Start a New TRADITION

For each card you send to a friend or family member, send one to a soldier deployed overseas or to someone in a hospice or retirement community in your area. Social media has made it easy for people to share Christmas-card campaigns to encourage those who are ill, so keep an eye out or even start a campaign of your own. Sometimes the slight time it takes to write in a card and send it can mean a lot to someone far from home or without family, and it's a great activity to do with children.

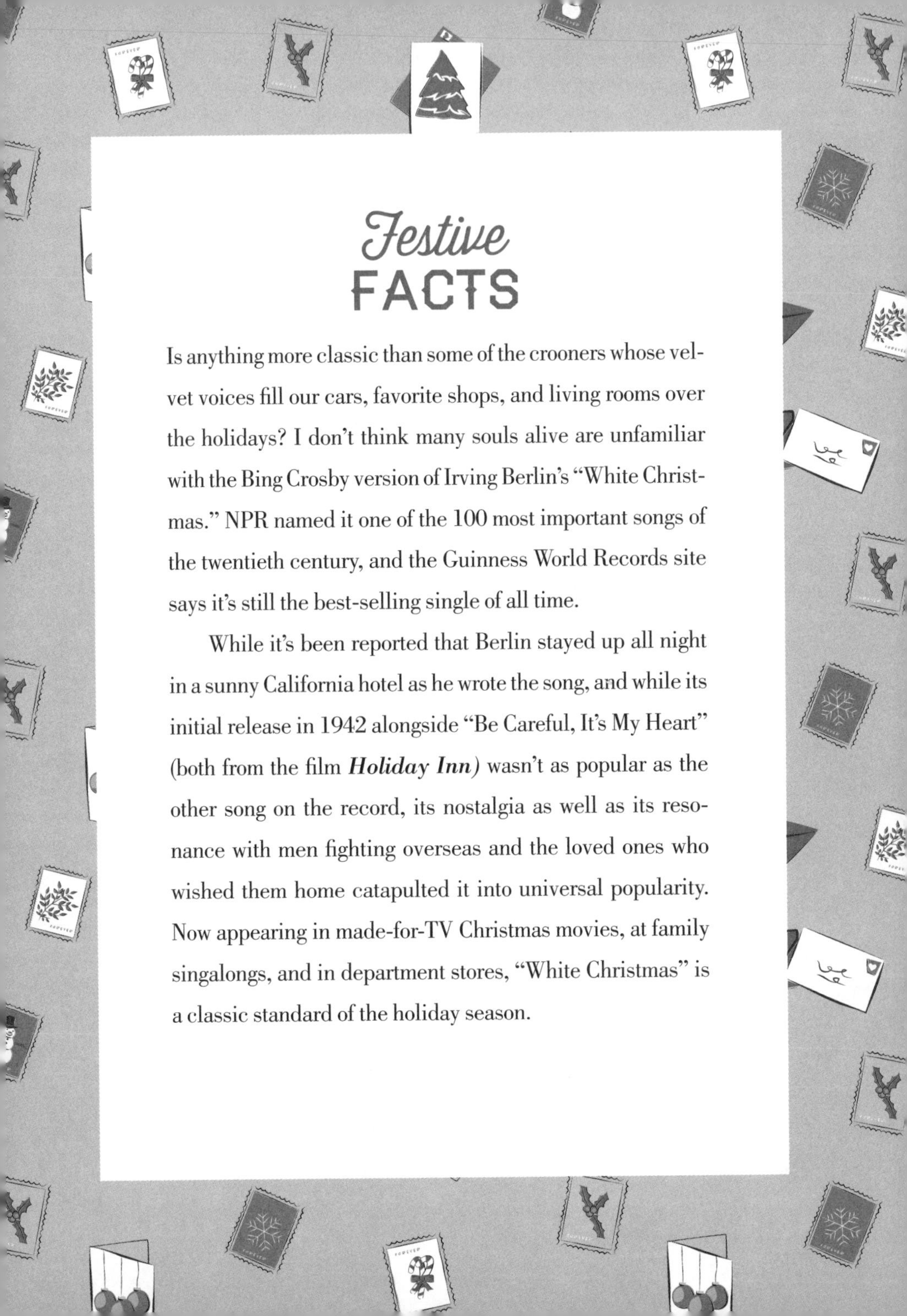

Festive FACTS

Is anything more classic than some of the crooners whose velvet voices fill our cars, favorite shops, and living rooms over the holidays? I don't think many souls alive are unfamiliar with the Bing Crosby version of Irving Berlin's "White Christmas." NPR named it one of the 100 most important songs of the twentieth century, and the Guinness World Records site says it's still the best-selling single of all time.

While it's been reported that Berlin stayed up all night in a sunny California hotel as he wrote the song, and while its initial release in 1942 alongside "Be Careful, It's My Heart" (both from the film ***Holiday Inn***) wasn't as popular as the other song on the record, its nostalgia as well as its resonance with men fighting overseas and the loved ones who wished them home catapulted it into universal popularity. Now appearing in made-for-TV Christmas movies, at family singalongs, and in department stores, "White Christmas" is a classic standard of the holiday season.

The Animal Lover's Christmas

Mountain lions actually take a leap of faith in love. When a male finds a female he's attracted to, he jumps in front of her, stopping her in her tracks.

THE NINE LIVES OF CHRISTMAS

Is there anything cuter than a dog with reindeer antlers or a kitten pawing at a low-hanging stocking? What about the gorgeous horses pulling a Christmas sleigh in a Currier and Ives print?

At no time of the year do I not love animals, but there's something magical in how they play into Christmas stories and legends. From the barnyard animals integral to the nativity scene to Rudolph and his lit nose—and even Sven, a reindeer who is Kristoff's best pal in the popular animated film franchise ***Frozen***—furry friends belong in our traditions. The wonder of a kid's imagination is always heightened at Christmastime, and for children who love to imagine their furry friends interacting with the season in a humanlike manner, it's the perfect time for stories featuring pets.

Whether the kids in your life like being the sheep in the Christmas pageant or accent their favorite seasonal sweaters with antlers and red noses, animals are one way to bring the family together at Christmas. While the first pet an adult had is behind many nostalgic memories, so the gift of a dog, cat, or fish over the holidays can lead to many new stories and responsibilities for the children in their lives. And keeping the memory of beloved pets from your childhood as well as making a usually pet-free house welcoming or visiting furry friends is an integral part of many peoples' Christmas experience. But even if you don't have the space or budget for your own animal, you can get creative at Christmas and ensure that animals are a part of your traditions.

No Pet? No Problem

Even without an animal of your own, you can ensure that the best season of the year features some cute creatures.

- 'Tis the season to help neighbors and friends with their Christmas loads. Offer to walk your neighbors' dog to give them more time to shop or get the turkey in the oven. If you have a friend or coworker who is planning a getaway over the holidays, offer to cat sit to save them finding a caregiver.
- Visiting or volunteering at the local Humane Society or animal shelter is a way for those without pets to engage with animals at Christmas.

At no time
of the year do I
not love animals,
but there's
something magical
in how they
play into
Christmas stories
and legends.

Customized VIEWING LIST

Adorable animals are at the heart of every recommended film below. Animals can often unintentionally bring their owners together, and a shared love of animals can establish an immediate kinship between a hero and heroine. A cute cat or dog not only provides an adorable costar to a star-studded Christmas cast but immediately stretches the viewing audience to include animal lovers.

- *The Nine Lives of Christmas:* A young veterinary student and a happily single firefighter fall immediately in love at Christmas when their cats meet.
- *12 Dog Days Till Christmas:* A troubled foster teen finds work at an animal shelter for Christmas, and the experience helps him appreciate his new family.
- *A Dogwalker's Christmas Tale:* College student Luce gets a holiday job caring for a land developer's dog, but when she meets Dean protesting her boss's plan to tear down the local dog park to build a ritzy spa, she is forced to consider how the spa would affect the community and her new friends.
- *The Dog Who Saved Christmas:* A police dog who has lost his bark and a man who has lost his way find their voices again during a memorable Christmas.

- *A Bride for Christmas:* A young woman whose passion is the dogs she raises at an animal shelter finds herself on the wrong side of a bet between male friends that one of them can woo her by Christmas. Furry friends are the perfect costars in this romantic movie.
- *Picture a Perfect Christmas:* A photographer returns home to tend to her elderly grandmother and ends up helping a neighbor take care of his nephew and a sweet rescue dog.

- Take your friends and family to a local farm or petting zoo—or even somewhere that offers a horse-drawn sleigh ride.

Christmas Photos and Pet Owners

If your best friends are your pets, Christmas can be a time to show them off in the best way. They can be the focus of a Christmas card photo or part of your family's photo. While pets might be notoriously hard to photograph, here are two tips to make it easier.

1. Don't expect too much of squirmy cats and excited dogs. Besides, sometimes the most charming and authentic photographs show the everyday chaos of life. But sounds, pictures, or videos on your phone can draw and keep an animal's attention while photographers work their magic. And waiting until after an exhausting walk or play session can make a rambunctious dog more amenable to sitting still.
2. Test canine accessories like reindeer antlers and Santa hats on pets beforehand so as not to surprise them at a photo session.

For the Animal-Loving Family

Incorporating animals into your Christmas traditions can inspire a fun and festive family outing.

- Often, churches will perform living nativity scenes featuring local animals such as sheep and donkeys, giving attendees an atmospheric and realistic sense of what the first Christmas was like.
- Create your own nativity scene for your fireplace mantel or another area in your home. While most nativity scenes are sold in sets with uniform-looking characters and animals, you can have your children select a barnyard menagerie to give a personal touch to your display.
- If you have a beloved pet that's likely to be anywhere near your Christmas tree, protect your most precious decorations by placing cheaper or decoy ornaments within its reach.

Start a New TRADITION

If you live in a neighborhood or apartment building with several cats and dogs, create tiny treat bags filled with kibble, chew bones, and squeaky toys to leave in mailboxes throughout the neighborhood or building—all from "Secret Santa."

Christmas is also a good time to think about your family engaging with animals too big for your house and unlikely to ever be in your neighborhood. Gift a spring day at the zoo as a stocking present. A day of trail riding or a private horseback lesson is another great gift experience that can allow members of your family to show their animal love at other times of the year.

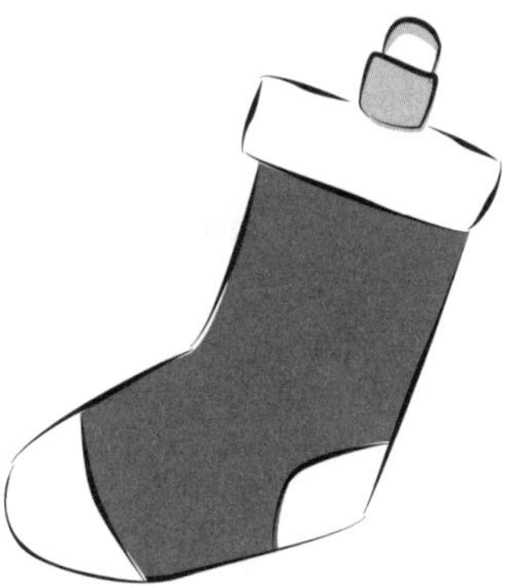

Festive FACTS

It's a well-known fact that Santa's sleigh is pulled by reindeer. And even before our modern version of Christmas reindeer came into being, the creatures were associated with St. Nicholas.

In nineteenth-century Germany, St. Nicholas was often depicted riding a horse or a donkey or riding in a chariot pulled by horses. But the Scandinavians were the first to introduce the concept of St. Nicholas's sleigh. This legend began to look a little more like what we know today because of the poem "A Visit from St. Nicholas," more widely known as "The Night Before Christmas." The eight reindeer pulling Santa's sleigh as he rode across the sky were introduced in that poem by Clement C. Moore. A century later, in 1939, the red-nosed reindeer guiding the sleigh for Santa, Rudolph, was introduced in the Gene Autry song, contributing to the popular folklore we recognize to this day.

The Old-Fashioned Christmas

You can listen to your mind,
but you have to follow your heart.

CHRISTMAS UNDER WRAPS

Every family has that old soul, the person who just seems to have the wisdom and insight of centuries. Also, the gal who would rather watch Masterpiece Theatre than the latest Hollywood blockbuster and is more comfortable prowling the internet for vintage clothes than shopping at the hottest store in the mall. The lover of Norman Rockwell prints who would rather (carefully and attentively) light candles perched on the tree than invest in the latest string of electric lights. Christmas is perfect for the history lover who wants to step into Christmas Past (ghosts not included).

Something about Christmas and ornaments makes us nostalgic for time periods we've never lived in. While Christmas in our world might require a perfect Instagram filter and our gifts might be sent via electronic cards that would puzzle most of the generations that came before us, the desire to return to the past and simpler times is

Something about Christmas and ornaments makes us nostalgic for time periods we've never lived in.

never heightened more than during the holidays. The songs we still sing and hear are sometimes hundreds of years old. (The most popular musical setting for "What Child Is This?" was registered as "Greensleeves" in 1580, though many believe the folk song existed long before that.) And the recipes we love are often replications of treats that precede us by centuries. While affixing lights to a tree is thought to have been started as early as Martin Luther's time, holly and ivy were mainstays in the courts of Queen Elizabeth I and her father, Henry VIII.

I believe our love for the old-fashioned and historic at Christmas allows us to feel closer to our ancestors, yes, but also to those who began the narrative of the traditions we love. This kind of celebration gives us a sense of awe to realize we're tasting recipes that, though they may sit so easily in our slow cookers, were once created on wrought-iron stoves. It allows us to revisit songs and stories that meant as much to their original listeners as they do to us. So let's turn off our modern appliances (except for the TV, of course), light some candles and a fire in the fireplace, and slip into the past.

The 12 Days of Christmas: A Primer

The origin of "The 12 Days of Christmas" comes from the centuries and traditions when Christmas season—or Twelvetide—was spread from the twenty-fifth of December (Christmas Day) to the fifth of January (eve of Epiphany—Epiphany remembering the arrival of the magi to visit the Christ child). As long ago as 567, when the Roman

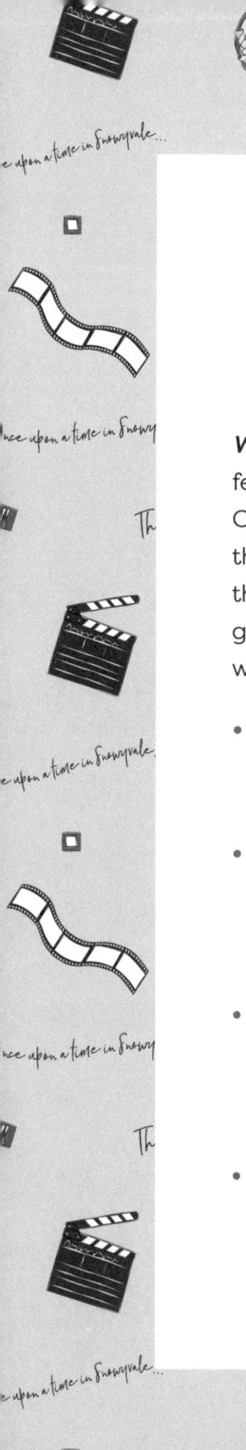

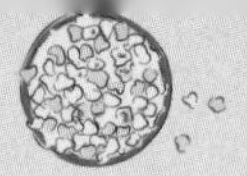

Customized VIEWING LIST

While ***It's a Wonderful Life***, ***White Christmas***, and ***The Man Who Invented Christmas*** are examples of perfect Hollywood features to get you in the mood for the season, made-for-TV Christmas movies also conjure the spirit of the past. Watching them will allow you to leave the bustle of your modern life on the doorstep and recall times of family, true friendship, gorgeous old homesteads, and ornaments and traditions that withstand the wearing of time.

- *Journey Back to Christmas:* A young World War II nurse is transported to the future and given a second chance, all while falling in love with a remarkable man.
- *The Christmas Card:* A soldier serving in Afghanistan is deeply moved by a Christmas card sent by a young woman doing a good deed, but will their love survive when they meet in person?
- *Christmas on Honeysuckle Lane:* In an attempt to honor her parents and remember Christmases past, a young woman revisits her childhood home and finds love in the most unexpectedly memorable way.
- *Christmas Land:* A career woman inherits her grandmother's beloved Christmas tree farm, but the more time she spends in the small town emulating the most old-fashioned of Christmas values and traditions, the less she wants to sell it for a sizable profit.

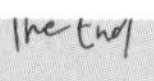
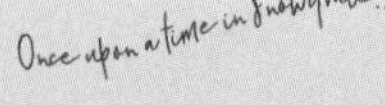

- *A Nutcracker Christmas:* Two dancers are reunited during rehearsals for a performance of the most famous ballet of all time, and when casting mishaps take place, they go from tutoring on the sidelines to taking center stage in a glorious Edwardian-era theater.
- *Nostalgic Christmas:* A young woman now working for a major city toy company returns home to her father's toy shop, which features perfect, old-fashioned, handmade wooden delights, and she realizes she doesn't miss the bells and whistles of her new life at all.

Catholic Council of Tours declared these days a sacred season, the dozen days were set apart as a time of feasting, merriment, religious remembrance, and gatherings.

On Twelfth Night, or the eve of Epiphany, entertainment, dining, and merriment were the norm—hence the title of the well-known Shakespeare play.

"The 12 Days of Christmas" speaks to this tradition through the presentation of increasingly affluent gifts from one admirer to his beloved. Although first published in 1780, there is evidence that the song was performed long before then. And while some have tried to impart religious or political meaning to the numbered stanzas, it's thought that the song is most likely a simple children's memory game.

Christmas Trivia

- Prince Albert of Germany, famous as the husband of Queen Victoria, introduced the Christmas tree we know today. The prince carried his home country's tradition of a Tanenbaum—a symbol that spring would soon return—into the British court, and by the height of the Victorian era, its popularity had spread, and people were decorating trees in their homes. Of course, the illustrations and popularity of Dickens's *A Christmas Carol*, written during the time of Victoria's reign, helped its popularity.
- From 1659 to 1681 in Boston, Massachusetts, Christmas was banned by Puritan observers. A fine was placed on those caught celebrating the season in their settlement.
- Good King Wenceslas of the carol by that name was an actual Bohemian duke known as Václav the Good and beloved by the inhabitants of Bohemia, the present Czech Republic. Renowned for his deep care for widows and orphans, as well as for his generosity to the poor and his religious piety, he was regarded as a saint and martyr immediately following his assassination by his power-hungry brother.

How to Roast the Perfect Chestnut (Without Burning Down Your House)

If you visited Christmas markets in many areas of the world, you would find the tradition of roasting and selling *maroni* (chestnuts) to keep customers' hands warm as they shop. They're often prepared over open fires in big barrels. To spare your home insurance, try making them in the oven.

Preheat the oven to 425°. For a half pound of chestnuts, use a paring knife to make an *X* shape on the round side of each chestnut (this keeps them from exploding due to the internal pressure of the oven heating).

Arrange the marked chestnuts on a baking tray and put it into the oven. Roast until the skins have pulled back from the *X*-marks (approximately 15 to 20 minutes). Remove and wrap the chestnuts in an old dish towel, squeezing them until they crackle.

Let them sit for a few minutes, then serve and enjoy!

Host a Regency-Era Christmas Brunch

Jane Austen is in constant demand even centuries after her books were published. While Christmas movies such as ***Sense, Sensibility & Snowmen***; ***Pride, Prejudice and Mistletoe***; and ***Christmas at Pemberley Manor*** update her classic stories to contemporary times, Austen lovers can use the viewing of these new classics as a springboard for a fun holiday get-together.

In Jane Austen's time and through to the Edwardian era, some

Jane Austen
is in constant
demand
even centuries
after her
books were
published.

of the most significant gatherings happened at breakfast. Breakfast was defined as the first true meal of the day, no matter what time it occurred, and it was often lavishly served. Readers of Jane Austen's books will remember that the large table settings in them, especially the morning after a ball, showed they were a staple of society. Revelers who had been dancing well past midnight before returning to their homes in the wee hours of the morning by coach would wake up far later than usual and in need of sustenance. A breakfast feast was often the preferred meal after a morning wedding as well, the newlyweds hosting a large midday meal before setting off on a wedding tour.

Of course, the offerings at these feasts differ from what we're accustomed to now, so while you might not want a whole suckling pig on your table, you can still re-create an Austen-era atmosphere with traditional fare. Hot chocolate to drink and poached or coddled eggs, brown bread, cheddar cheese, and cold meats are some offerings you can feature to help establish a sense of authenticity. You might not want to eat kippers or salt herring in the morning either, but smoked salmon makes a nice alternative.

Create an Old-Fashioned Christmas Invitation

Invite your guests to brunch with homemade "parchment" papers, emulating the type of invitation a young Austen heroine such as Emma would have received for a Highbury Christmas Ball. Here's how:

- Use your best calligraphy skills or print out desired text on a plain sheet of white paper.
- Place two black tea bags in a mug and steep with boiling water.
- Squeeze the excess liquid from the tea bags and begin to dab them over the paper (don't forget to flip to the other side). Make sure some areas are uneven to give the paper an even older feel. (Tip: Turmeric and coffee grounds can be employed to help weather the page even more.)
- Use a candle to burn some of the edges so the paper will look all the more old-fashioned.
- Tie each invitation with a ribbon after rolling it into a scroll or fold it and then seal it with a stamp.

I guarantee most local theaters and community groups will be presenting something old-fashioned during the Christmas season. Take the family to a local production of *The Nutcracker* or a public reading of O. Henry's "The Gift of the Magi." Churches and choirs often offer Handel's *Messiah*, an oratorio long appropriated by the Christmas season. *A Christmas Carol* either read dramatically or performed on stage is a wonderful way to evoke Christmases past. If you can't attend a performance out, consider the many audio and radio versions of these works available for modern listeners.

Festive FACTS

Christmas icons and symbols are part of the wonder of the season. From Rudolph's red nose to Frosty the Snowman's top hat, they loan a fun and whimsical spirit to the season. In many cultures around the world, St. Nicholas is portrayed as a regal figure. Sure, he's benevolent, but just as the Dutch *Sinterklaas* is accompanied by *Zwarte Piet* (Black Peter), who will leave lumps of coal in the shoes of naughty children, so the German and Austrian St. Nicholas is accompanied by *Krampus*, a scary horned figure who reminds children to stay in line.

Both are a far cry from the jolly St. Nick in North American traditions, and we largely have Coca-Cola to thank for it. For many years St. Nicholas was portrayed as a lean and distant figure—even without any frightening figures accompanying him. But in 1931, the Coca-Cola company hired an illustrator named Haddon Sundblom to create an image of Santa for their Christmas campaign. His jolly, rotund, and bright figure was a contrast to the Depression currently plaguing America, and Santa happily holding a Coke bottle is one of the most iconic advertising images to this day.

The Fashion Lover's Christmas

It's not about what you need; it's about what you wish for.

CHRISTMAS IN HOMESTEAD

If you have watched as many made-for-TV Christmas movies as I have, you have probably noticed certain trends. One is to name heroines Eve, Holly, Ivy, Noelle, or Belle in keeping with festive themes. Another is to ensure that what is on the screen at any given moment reflects the season. Ideally, each frame should provide a Christmassy vignette. As such, we're given a merry canvas of red and green, gold and silver, and the whitest of snow. Sometimes this backdrop is provided by well-decorated sets, other times by the coordination of the actors' clothes with the season.

Christmas is a fashion lover's paradise. We have work parties, family functions, shindigs, and other opportunities to pull out the ugly Christmas sweaters we love, but we can also take chances not so hideous. The formal dress hiding at the back of our closet throughout the year may finally suit an upcoming function, and the sparkle and glitter we're eager to wear are not out of place at events that glisten!

I look at Christmas as a time when wearing reindeer antlers is acceptable and Santa hats can be staple accessories for shopping or an office party. No one will look at you twice (if they do so, it will be with a smile) if you wear shoes with elf-points, and the gaudier the earrings or jinglier the necklace, the better. We decorate our mantels! We decorate our trees! And Christmas gives fashion lovers a chance to decorate themselves in the brightest, most whimsical manner possible.

So whether you're more comfortable in a dress in the style Rosemary Clooney wears in ***White Christmas***, or that hoodie you found with a gimmicky, battery-operated reindeer nose that lights up is more your style, make Christmas your own by being festive both inside ***and*** outside.

How to Dress like a Christmas Movie Heroine

Made-for-TV Christmas movies most often have an intentional palette of red, green, and white. While outside shots feature snow and charming hometowns decorated for the holidays, the living rooms and cozy kitchens always feature colors synonymous with the season as well.

The wardrobes of the heroines are just as intentional, and they're often coordinated to suit the Christmas canvas the film is creating. In ***Sense, Sensibility & Snowmen***, the heroine, Elinor, wears festive scarves to show her love of the season (a particularly

I look at Christmas
as a time when
wearing
reindeer antlers
is acceptable and
Santa hats
can be staple
accessories for
shopping
or an office party.

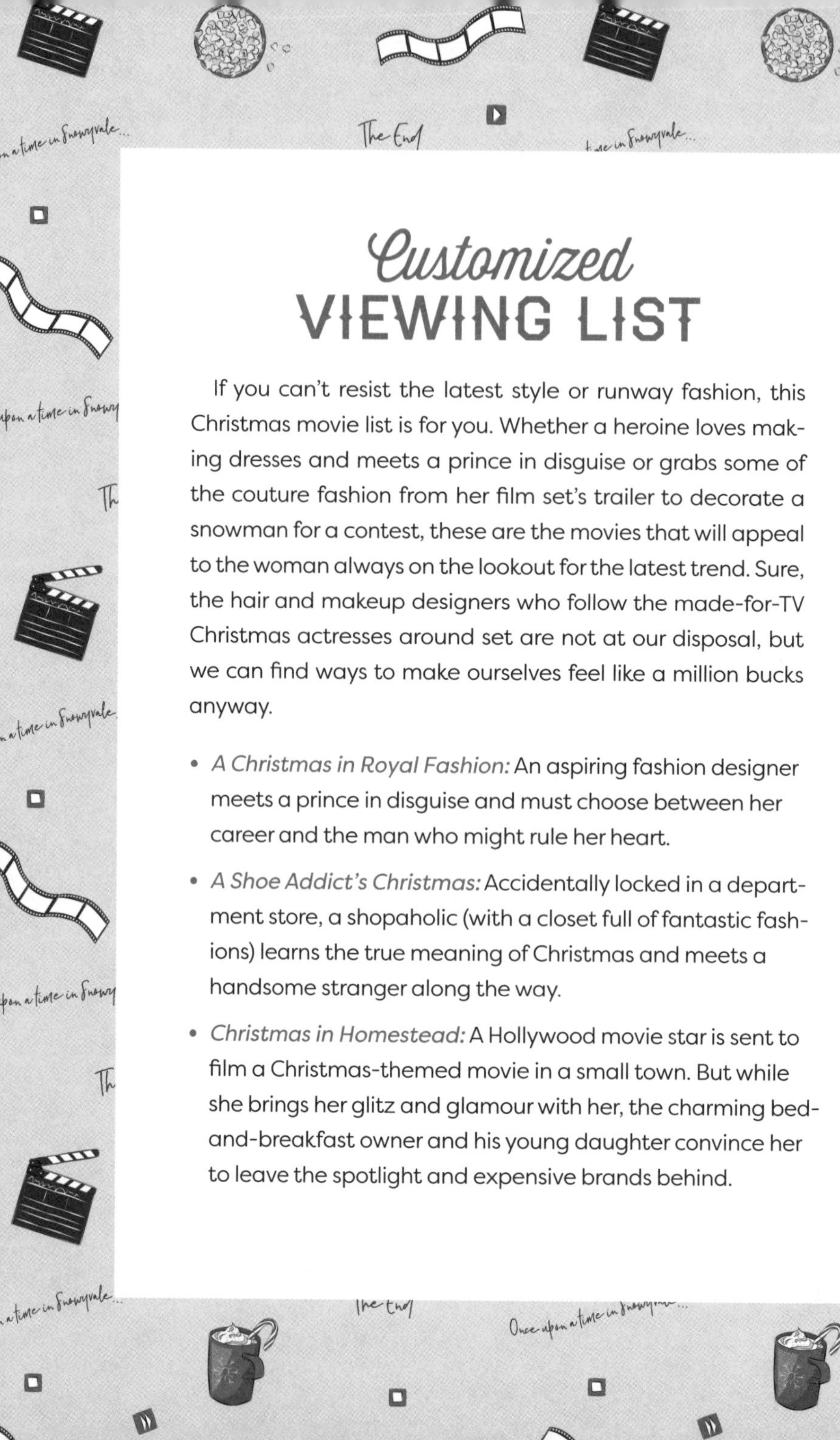

Customized VIEWING LIST

If you can't resist the latest style or runway fashion, this Christmas movie list is for you. Whether a heroine loves making dresses and meets a prince in disguise or grabs some of the couture fashion from her film set's trailer to decorate a snowman for a contest, these are the movies that will appeal to the woman always on the lookout for the latest trend. Sure, the hair and makeup designers who follow the made-for-TV Christmas actresses around set are not at our disposal, but we can find ways to make ourselves feel like a million bucks anyway.

- *A Christmas in Royal Fashion:* An aspiring fashion designer meets a prince in disguise and must choose between her career and the man who might rule her heart.
- *A Shoe Addict's Christmas:* Accidentally locked in a department store, a shopaholic (with a closet full of fantastic fashions) learns the true meaning of Christmas and meets a handsome stranger along the way.
- *Christmas in Homestead:* A Hollywood movie star is sent to film a Christmas-themed movie in a small town. But while she brings her glitz and glamour with her, the charming bed-and-breakfast owner and his young daughter convince her to leave the spotlight and expensive brands behind.

- *A Royal Christmas:* A seamstress hangs up her dress designs in exchange for the opportunity to spend Christmas with the charming heir to the throne.
- *Road to Christmas:* The producer of a lifestyle network show with a great fashion savvy is charged with a holiday make-over that leads her to her true love.

adorable snowman pattern catches the eye of the hero), and in ***Our Christmas Love Song***, the heroine closes out her big finale in a Christmas concert wearing a flared red sateen dress that recalls Christmases past.

To dress like a made-for-TV Christmas movie heroine, you'll need the following:

- the confidence to take the season to the next level fashion-wise
- red, green, white, and gold dresses or sweaters
- candy-cane striped nylons
- chunky ivory knit sweaters with sleeves just long enough to drape over your hands as you hold a steamy cup of cocoa
- a poinsettia brooch from a deceased relative whose Christmas tree farm you're this close to saving
- a flimsy wrap over your formal wear that does so little to dispel the winter chill as you walk arm in arm from the town hall lighting ceremony with your dashing hero that he has no choice but to loan you his suit

jacket or plaid lumberjack coat (depending on where you are)

- a snuggly jeans-and-sweats wardrobe that will contrast brilliantly with your final, big reveal on the winding staircase of a prince's castle, draped in a bright-red, floor-length gown that perfectly matches your glittery, snowflake-styled tiara (bonus points if your name is Merry, Eve, Ivy, Noelle, Joy, or Belle)

From Ugly Christmas Sweater to Christmas Chic

Few occasions call for the most dastardly piece of clothing we own, but ugly Christmas sweater parties and gatherings have become a mainstay of many traditions. While most are manufactured specifically for the season in all of their garish cheesiness, the trend began with people wearing unintentionally humorous clothing gifted to them.

The shock of a good ugly Christmas sweater delights many people, but the prospect of spending a lot of money on a gimmick item they'll wear in only one season of the year doesn't thrill the people who would like to be seen in one. The best way to find the desired Christmas sweater without much expense is to frequent rummage sales and Salvation Army stores, Goodwill Stores, and other charity and thrift shops throughout the year (the pickings will be slim by December 1 due to other avid hunters). If you find a neighborhood garage sale, you might have luck there as well.

If you're crafty and enjoy knitting, try to find some old patterns

Consider purchasing a dress in a single color you can also use for other occasions and then dress it up or down.

for a sweater you can make in a color and scheme long out of fashion. Start early enough, and you'll have the perfect, unique wardrobe for your next Christmas party.

If you don't want to pull out the same sweater every year, consider hosting an ugly Christmas sweater swap. This sustainable and fun event will have you and your friends trading sweaters so you can all happily surprise your next gathering.

How to Dress for a Christmas Party

Going from a day at the office to an after-work Christmas party could mean changing clothes in the stalls of the office restroom. Or it might just mean taking a few simple steps to elevate your look from day to night—and spending a lot of money on one party doesn't have to be your only option.

If you don't want to go all out buying a dress just for a Christmas party, consider purchasing a dress in a single color you can also use for other occasions and then dress it up or down. Perhaps a white sweater dress or slightly off-the-shoulder black dress would suit boots and tights for one event but red heels for another.

- Accessories can go a long way to making an outfit festive, but they also draw the eye away from your clothing, which is especially nice if you've worn it to an office party before.

- Speaking of accessories...sparkly earrings, a Christmas-patterned scarf, or even a pop of color by way of red or green heels or ankle boots can dress up an outfit for the season and make it stand out.
- A white, sparkly blazer can elevate a plain dress yet keep it classic, and grabbing a bow or ribbon peeking out of your Christmas wrapping box can make for an inexpensive and fun hair accessory.
- Consider using a favorite, classic, crystal ornament as a brooch and even investing in a few pairs of Christmas-themed earrings.

A Christmas Movie Heroine's Capsule Wardrobe

- a festive scarf
- a knit hat with a pompom
- the ugly Santa or Frosty the Snowman sweater your mom made you wear in high school so the hero can make good-natured fun of you
- fashionable boots that withstand even the most intense winter blizzard
- matching pj's and fuzzy slippers to wear during midnight cookie baking

- a full-length ball gown and long gloves for the holiday ball you didn't know you were attending ahead of time yet magically seem to have—as well as the appropriate heels and undergarments
- an overnight bag that, despite your capsule wardrobe tendencies, is as roomy as Mary Poppins's and holds a wardrobe big enough for a week while snow-stranded in a small town like Wild Firs, Connecticut. A Christmas movie heroine also brings several winter coats and an array of scarves and gloves, as well as at least two pairs of boots.

Instead of rushing out to buy that new holiday outfit, repurpose clothing items you already have. You might even enjoy hosting a festive clothing swap just before the holiday parties begin so you and your friends can shop from one another's closets and find new-to-you outfits and accessories to wear to the season's social functions.

In the spirit of giving, declutter Christmas by making the weeks leading up to it an opportunity to purge the unwanted (yet in good condition) clothes you have from the year before and gifting them to a woman's shelter.

While the Coca-Cola company certainly helped spread the version of Santa currently beloved in North America, we can also credit illustrator Thomas Nast for his version of St. Nicholas in an 1870 portrait to align with "A Visit from St. Nicholas." While earlier versions of the European St. Nicholas had shown the figure clothed in red (a traditionally regal color), the cap and fuzzy sleeves we know today can be traced to the nineteenth century as well as recall the prosperous Ghost of Christmas Yet to Come in the Dickens tale.

For a long time, candy canes were a staple for children at Christmas but presented ivory white. The earliest appearance of a staffed candy cane is attributed to a choirmaster in seventeenth-century Cologne, Germany, who gifted children candy in the shape of the staffs the shepherds carried in the Bible story. By the nineteenth century, with the growing popularity of Christmas trees, the hooked end of the cane allowed for easy hanging and decoration. And by the early twentieth century, it was nearly impossible to find candy canes without the addition of red and green stripes.

The Family Christmas

The smallest stone makes a ripple in the water.

JOURNEY BACK TO CHRISTMAS

My happiest memories are from Christmastime, including the ones I have of my grandpa and my aunt, who have now passed. I don't remember what no doubt went wrong; I remember only the warmth and magic. Perhaps our memories put a protective bubble around the season to preserve its best moments—especially when it comes to recalling loved ones who are no longer with us—because I can guarantee you, my childhood Christmases didn't look like the perfect movie sets we see in the Christmas movies we love.

On Christmas morning, we would all peek inside our stockings without wearing matching pj's and with our hair sticking up in all directions. Our overtired and excited natures probably led my brother, sister, and me to snap at each other. With aunts and uncles around, the house was often crowded, and in no time, I'm sure crumpled wrapping paper and empty glasses were strewn everywhere, the morning's breakfast dishes still piled in the sink.

I don't

remember

what no doubt

went wrong;

I remember

only the

warmth and

magic.

I don't recall any of that. I don't remember little arguments or the years I didn't get the presents I asked for. I remember the recipes—my mom's spinach dip and her turkey dinner, the shortbread cookies my aunt loved, my aunt's family-famous cheeseball. I remember the traditions—the singing, my grandpa in charge of passing out gifts. (Well, I do remember the agony of waiting through the Christmas service at church, knowing that presents were awaiting us at home. But the imperfection of Christmas made it all the more exciting.)

I think we sometimes set unrealistic expectations for what the holiday should be and how perfectly every last plan needs to be executed. If our home doesn't look Pinterest worthy, if our presents aren't wrapped and placed under the tree with the same, consistent brilliance we see in the Christmas movies on our TVs, we feel as if we've failed.

At its heart, though, Christmas is about family.

So let's take the pressure off. Let us all—each grandmother, mom, aunt, daughter, sister, niece, and girlfriend—focus more on cherishing the moments with those we love than aiming for perfection. Christmas comes with unique and special opportunities to capture moments the people around us will remember even as we all grow older and schedules change.

Customized VIEWING LIST

Made-for-TV Christmas movies place the love and light of family at their core. From stories about sisters being reunited at Christmastime, to single fathers finding true love, to neighbors and friends forging a family not bound by blood, holiday movies respect the importance of familial units.

A popular trope in made-for-TV Christmas movies imagines heroes or heroines offered the chance to view their lives as if they had been granted their big promotion or some other significant personal opportunity and taken it even at the expense of their family. Alternatively, characters who have made the decision to pursue a high-profile work life are given the opportunity to wake up in a different life, as if they had married their high school sweetheart and enjoyed a slower pace with a white picket fence and kids rehearsing for the Christmas pageant. And while sometimes characters bring fake girlfriends or boyfriends to family gatherings in hopes of stopping the incessant questions about their marital status, there's no doubt that the heart of Christmas is family.

- *November Christmas:* A devastating diagnosis for a young girl inspires her kind neighbors and family to reboot the calendar so she can experience every favorite holiday one last time.

- *Trading Christmas:* A house swap finds a single mother enjoying an urban Christmas in Boston with a handsome new beau while a grouchy writer is pulled out of his shell by a feisty travel agent—both learning that family is the most important part of the holidays.
- *The Christmas Secret:* An act of goodwill offsets a series of unforgettable Christmas moments for a kindhearted single mother and the man she was destined to be with.
- *Family for Christmas:* A workaholic investigative journalist is granted a wish to experience Christmas with a family and learns she wouldn't go back to the freedom of her own life for any reason.
- *Christmas with Holly:* A six-year-old girl finds love and hope after her mother's death when she's cared for by her three bachelor uncles.

Embrace a Family Christmas

Family outings at Christmas can be difficult considering busy schedules and the stress of the season. But immediate families should make time for one another even before all of the guests and friends arrive. Consider the following ways you can ensure family time is treasured:

- A pizza and movie night complete with new pj's or slippers and a holiday movie everyone votes for is a great way to share time together.
- Assign a number of ornaments to each member of the family, making them responsible for hanging them each year. If school events, sports teams, business travel, or any other commitments keep someone from being present at the actual tree decorating, they'll still know they'll be part of the tradition by hanging their assigned ornaments later.
- Each year, plan a family Christmas shopping trip. Part of the fun will be every member keeping their purchases from the eyes of others.
- As part of a Christmas shopping trip, visit a store that sells ornaments and allow each family member to choose one for the family tree and one for themselves. This way the tradition and narrative of Christmases past are married with new ones.
- Together, watch home movies from Christmases past.

Master a Stress-Free Christmas

- If it becomes too expensive and too stressful to accommodate every person on your family's Christmas list, draw names so each person is charged with only one person to buy for—with a set spending limit.
- Plan a potluck so you're not making all the food for an extended family Christmas gathering yourself, allowing everyone to contribute to the fun.
- A family celebration doesn't need to be held on Christmas Day to be special. If flights and schedules keep everyone from making it for the twenty-fifth, remember it's not so much the date as the *people* making Christmas a special holiday.

Create a Build-a-Snowman Kit

When you find garage sales and sale bins throughout the year, keep an eye out for items to create a snowman kit for the whole family.

- mismatched buttons for eyes and noses
- hats like top hat for a snowman and a netted vintage hat for a snowwoman
- scarves
- mittens
- boots
- accessories such as an umbrella or cane

Start a New TRADITION

Give the busy mom in your life a Christmas surprise. Offer free babysitting so she can get some last-minute shopping done. Make a meal or two or offer to do the Christmas cookie baking for her kids' school event to lessen her load.

Find ways to help other families in need, even if it means going out of your way to do it. Contact a local charity, such as the Salvation Army, to see if they have a program to help give those experiencing a harder-than-normal year a good Christmas. Or set up a program in your church that takes into consideration everything a family would need for an amazing Christmas dinner. To that end, establish a "Build a Christmas Box" program where families can contribute groceries, goodies, festive decorations, and warm clothing to give someone who will appreciate it most.

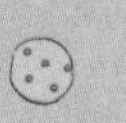

Nollaig na mBan, or Women's Little Christmas, is an Irish tradition most popular in Cork and Kerry. It arrives every year on January 6—the Feast of the Epiphany. On this day, men are charged with the household chores, giving the women in their lives a much-needed break from the work they've put into hosting and baking over the holidays. Restaurant reservations are still mostly made by women on this day, and mothers, sisters, and girlfriends gather together to celebrate and exchange gifts in the spirit of recognizing everything women have done to pull off a successful holiday season.

The Romantic's Christmas

I'm the girl who loves family. I'm the girl who loves romance and antiques and history. But most of all, I'm the girl who loves you.

A VERY MERRY MIX-UP

Is anything more romantic than a roaring fire, two cups of cocoa with marshmallows piled high, a shared blanket, and an Ella Fitzgerald Christmas classic on Spotify? Christmas is definitely a season of love. Everyone is in a good mood, there are parties and mingling galore, and the guy you crush on at the office shows a cute and humorous side when he wears that reindeer sweater his grandma knit for him. But sometimes Christmas and romance can remind all the single ladies of either their lack of a special someone or a past Christmas shared with a past love.

The good news is that whether or not you have a special someone in your life, the romance of Christmas is meant to be enjoyed by everyone. Why not create a memorable romantic experience for you and some girlfriends by making a Christmas movie viewing

The good news
is that whether or
not you have
a special someone
in your life,
the romance of
Christmas is meant
to be enjoyed by
everyone.

experience a night to remember? You can even use a free design website such as Canva or PicMonkey to create the perfect festive e-vite for your event as well as curate the perfect movie and ambience.

This isn't just having a few girls over for popcorn and a romantic movie. This is a themed event that can re-create the magic of a favorite Christmas movie. In most romantic Christmas TV movies, the small town and rural settings include a picture-perfect holiday café where the hero and heroine get to know each other over pastries and coffee. Or the heroine discusses her new love interest with her best friend over a candy-cane latte. Re-create this moment in your kitchen or dining room with your own Christmas café.

Create a Christmas Movie Café

Here's what you'll need for your own Christmas movie café:

- candles scented in caramel, candy cane, gingerbread, or pine
- a checkered or festive tablecloth or holiday napkins
- inexpensive artificial holly, pine cones, and garlands found at the dollar store to make a festive centerpiece
- a holiday apron
- decorated menus that include festive tea, hot chocolate, and coffee you can serve

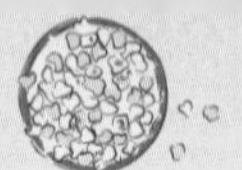

Customized VIEWING LIST

The recommended movies for this chapter are full of romantic plots that will make you sigh and swoon. From the young woman who ends up at the wrong house for Christmas and falls for a man who shares her love for antiques to a couple who meet on an online dating app that matches singles just for holiday events, the titles below are the perfect customized viewing list to watch with your girlfriends as you do your nails or trim the tree.

- *The Father Christmas trilogy* (*Finding Father Christmas, Engaging Father Christmas, Marrying Father Christmas*): In the first of this heart-warming trilogy from Robin Jones Gunn, a young woman finds love and community in a quest to reconnect with her actress mother and locate the father she's never known.
- *A Very Merry Mix-Up:* A young woman believes she's meeting her new fiancé's family for the holidays, but when she ends up at the wrong house, she finds herself falling for the man she believes to be her future brother-in-law.
- *The Christmas Ornament:* A widow is given her deceased husband's blessing to fully celebrate the holidays through the gift of a timeless ornament just as a new love interest arrives in her life.

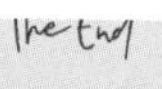
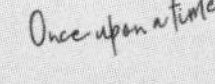

- *Mingle All the Way:* In the age of online dating, what better app for a single woman than one that pairs you with an immediate date for family functions, where—especially at Christmas—you'll face the inevitable questions about your couple status? But what if that app leads you to the man of your dreams?
- *The Knight Before Christmas:* A schoolteacher disillusioned about love learns a lesson in medieval chivalry when a knight is transported to her modern classroom at Christmas.

your guests as requested (brewed coffee or hot chocolate garnished with whipped cream, sprinkles, candy canes, cinnamon sticks, or marshmallows is an easy way to turn a hot beverage into a festive treat)

- a Christmas playlist

Make a Girls'-Night-In Kit

Here's what you'll need for this fun kit:

- red, green, and gold nail polish and festive emery boards (check Walmart, Target, and Amazon for favorite designs)
- individual facial masks
- fuzzy socks
- dark chocolate
- candy canes
- individual cocoa packets
- the link to a Spotify holiday playlist made specifically for your guests
- holiday-scented tea lights

Make an Eggnog Latte

Gather enough ingredients for one perfect cup, but increase the ingredient amounts if you have company, depending on how many latte lovers you're serving.

- ½ cup eggnog
- ¼ cup milk
- 1 T. sugar (or to taste)
- ¼ cup brewed espresso or very strong coffee
- Whipped cream, for on top
- Nutmeg, for sprinkling on the whipped cream

Brew the coffee/espresso and place in a mug.

In a small pan, pour in the eggnog, milk, and sugar. Whisk together over medium heat until hot and frothy, about 2 to 3 minutes. Pour the combination into the mug with the coffee. Garnish with whipped cream and nutmeg as desired.

One cup

Start a New TRADITION

Preface your girls' night in with a new Christmas tradition—volunteering. As a group, offer to work at a homeless shelter, a soup kitchen, an elementary school serving a turkey dinner, or to read to people in a hospice facility or retirement community.

Instead of having a pre-Christmas gift exchange, organize a post-Christmas gift exchange and spread the fun into the new year. Hit up the post-Christmas sales at your favorite gift and decor stores and give your friends an item they can add to next year's Christmas decorations.

Festive FACTS

A lady would be fortunate to have a man willing to shower as many thoughtful holiday gifts on her as is bestowed in the beloved "The Twelve Days of Christmas." From golden rings to swans and geese, nothing seems left out of this benevolent (and seemingly unending) series of gifts. But to me, one of the most meaningful gifts is the turtle dove, which represents several qualities someone would look for not only in a romantic partner but also in a friend. In the Bible, doves are a symbol of peace but also of hope. After all, Noah releases a dove from his ark during the flood to find dry land and the promise that his family's hardship is over. White doves symbolize purity, and all doves symbolize friendship, maternal care, and love as well. Piping pipers and leaping lords are all well and good, but I love the symbolism behind these beautiful birds.

The Destination Christmas

As I was sipping on my coffee waiting to board,
I remembered that you said you loved me,
and I realized that you mean it.

I'M NOT READY FOR CHRISTMAS

The anticipation preceding visiting family and road trips to our favorite places makes the holidays special. Bundling up in the car with the heater on and Christmas tunes on the radio, all with the prospect of seeing loved ones at the end of the journey, is part of the magic of Christmas. When I was a little girl, one of my favorite smells was of the cold and snow sticking to the coats of my aunts and uncles as they first stepped into our home for Christmas, and I would wait by the window watching for their cars. Now I love the final moments before I pull into the drive to see my nieces and nephew. The distance that separates people during the year can seem awfully far in the last miles before we reach someone's driveway. And the promise of excitement, warmth, love, and goodies once we're there is captured so well in made-for-TV Christmas movies.

Some people may decide to travel to a faraway location,

budgeting throughout the year so they can experience Christmas across the sea, while others may decide to experience Christmas in a new way without leaving their county or state. No matter what you choose, the holidays can be a fantastic time to step out of the usual. For example, you can explore that nearby museum or homestead you usually can't squeeze into your schedule. They might even inspire you to somehow bring a foreign destination into your home.

Travel in Style

Hayrides and sleigh rides are popular around the holiday season. If you live in a rural area or within driving distance of an orchard or farms, start there. They're usually the best bet for these types of services. To save on cost and spread the joy, look into group rates and invite people from your church, book club, or school to come and bring their families.

Visiting European Christmas markets is a fantastic holiday getaway to get in the festive mood while also experiencing a new culture. From Tallinn, Estonia, to Nuremburg, Germany, Christmas markets are a centuries-old tradition that allow vendors from

The distance
that separates
people during the
year can seem
awfully far in the
last miles before we
reach someone's
driveway.

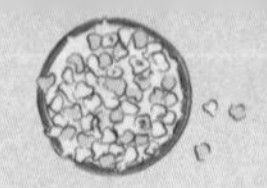

Customized VIEWING LIST

Road trip movies with beautiful locales can inspire you to spend the holidays somewhere beautiful, places you've never experienced. Not only does the adventure of navigating something new make for the best memories, but the romantic in me loves the prospect of meeting a fabulous person who is also enjoying a new setting. The magic of travel—near or far—is that visiting an unfamiliar place immediately gives you something in common.

Often, the most romantic Christmas stories, like some of the ones in the movies I've listed here, are born of a weather mishap—being snowed in for Christmas or rerouted during travel due to a storm. Then sparks fly when the characters learn to adapt to the journey they're on, finding the magic in the spirit of those who help them find a temporary sense of home for the holiday. But no matter the destination—planned or not—we can revel in the journey they encounter once there.

- *A Christmas Detour:* When a bridal magazine editor is waylaid on route to meet her wealthy fiancé and in-laws, and then flights are canceled, she must rely on the kindness of strangers in western New York to get to New York City. The cynical no-nonsense man who offers her a ride inspires her to take a look at her life across the miles.

- *Enchanted Christmas:* A warm climate, a ballroom, and salsa dancing are at the heart of this romantic film set against the renovation of a beloved old inn in Sante Fe, New Mexico.
- *Snowed-Inn Christmas:* Two rival travel writers need to rethink their holiday plans when a snowstorm strands them in a small town—Santa Claus, Indiana—that reminds them of a Christmas card.
- *Poinsettias for Christmas:* What says Christmas like a poinsettia farm—no matter where that farm is? This floral-featured movie is the perfect way to escape into a greenhouse and learn about the care and nurture of flowers. Their care takes the magic touch of a young woman returning to her roots and a new farmer who might be able to help her find the heart of her childhood again.
- *Debbie Macomber's Dashing Through the Snow:* When two strangers need to share a car to get to their Christmas destinations in Seattle, they find themselves the inadvertent owners of a puppy, tailed by the FBI, and falling in love along the way.

faraway rural regions to bring their wares to sell in populous urban centers. In Vienna, the Christmas markets feature the delicate woodcarvings of artists from the Tyrolean Alps, and in Prague, glass makers from across the Czech Republic bring their fragile pieces.

You can even bring Christmas markets to the comfort of your own town or city. At a Christmas fundraiser, for instance, re-create the popular European Christkindl markets, a staple of Christmas in several countries, including Austria and Germany. Set up booths and kiosks to mirror the ones spread throughout European town squares, where people can sell crafts and cards, knitwear and ornaments. Don't forget stations that offer Christmas goodies and hot drinks. And you can keep this European tradition: Have those who buy a drink also place a suitably priced deposit on the Christmas-themed mug their beverage is served in. If they return the mug before they leave, they get the deposit back. If not, they take home a souvenir, and your fundraiser makes a profit.

Travel Tip: If you want to experience world-famous European Christmas markets on a budget, consider booking airfare and hotels for mid-November, when most of the markets first open. You'll get off-season booking prices as well as avoid the crowds closer to Christmas.

Take Christmas Day Trips

Maybe you can't afford either the time or expense to travel far, but Christmas-themed day trips can offer a fun alternative.

- Check out the holiday lights, community Christmas tree, and decorated shop windows in a nearby city or town.
- Instead of buying your Christmas tree from the lot you frequent every year, make choosing your tree an adventure by visiting a lot in a new area.
- Depending on where you live, visiting Christmas tree or poinsettia farms and greenhouses can offer an exciting adventure.

Traveling need not mean raking up a ton of mileage in your car. Many churches have parishioners no longer able to transport themselves to Christmas services or concerts in their community. Talk to your pastor about how you could volunteer to drive those people to such events and what the security background checks would be. Make the experience fun for your passengers by dressing up in festive gear, offering them a candy cane or other treat, and ensuring carols are sung en route to your destination.

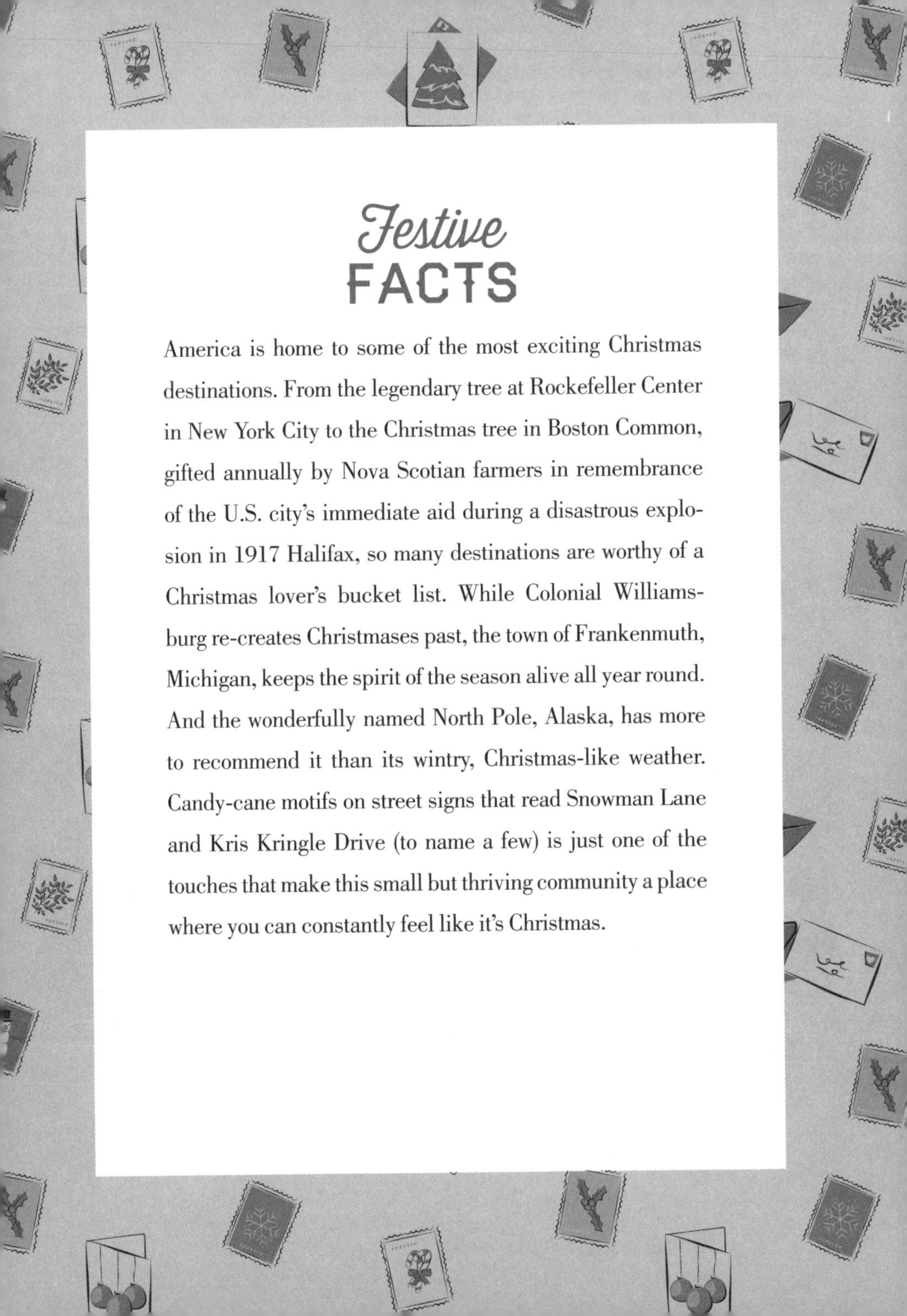

Festive FACTS

America is home to some of the most exciting Christmas destinations. From the legendary tree at Rockefeller Center in New York City to the Christmas tree in Boston Common, gifted annually by Nova Scotian farmers in remembrance of the U.S. city's immediate aid during a disastrous explosion in 1917 Halifax, so many destinations are worthy of a Christmas lover's bucket list. While Colonial Williamsburg re-creates Christmases past, the town of Frankenmuth, Michigan, keeps the spirit of the season alive all year round. And the wonderfully named North Pole, Alaska, has more to recommend it than its wintry, Christmas-like weather. Candy-cane motifs on street signs that read Snowman Lane and Kris Kringle Drive (to name a few) is just one of the touches that make this small but thriving community a place where you can constantly feel like it's Christmas.

The Homebody's Christmas

We've all lost something or someone that we love in this world, and someone else's happy Christmas can make it hurt all over again if we don't let Christmas do what it was meant to do.

SIGNED, SEALED, DELIVERED FOR CHRISTMAS

There's a reason the phrase *Home for Christmas* is embroidered on so many accent pillows. There's a reason "(There's No Place Like) Home for the Holidays" is crooned through our radio speakers and department store sound systems. Christmas is a time of warmth, nostalgia, and family, and we might feel the need for home—or at least the memory of what we feel is our *true* home—during the holiday more than at any other season of the year.

Often, we associate *home* with where our family lives. While I certainly cherish my time at Christmas with my parents, in their home where I grew up, and the celebrations at my aunt's and siblings' homes, my Christmas also finds me in my tiny apartment in the city. That's because even though I love my family and our collective Christmas traditions, I treasure the traditions I've cultivated myself. I treasure being a homebody. This includes frequenting my favorite Toronto Christmas markets and the tallest and most elaborately decorated Christmas trees, but it also means embellishing my apartment with my own Christmas touches, including the tree ornaments I've collected from friends, family, and adventures.

Thinking of home can sometimes be painful, though. The first few Christmases after I lost my beloved Aunt Sylvia were difficult. I didn't see how I could fill the major gap in the holiday with anything but *her*. But as the holidays came and went, I realized her memory was most potent at Christmas because I made it so. I took time to sit and remember her. I didn't feel the need, necessarily, to share those memories (though any conversation where her name organically came up was special and wonderful); rather, I intentionally carved out a space at Christmas to remember my time with her in my favorite season.

Your homebody Christmas may be the result of the loss of a loved one, but it can also be born of a need to get to know yourself again. To try a new recipe. To test out traditions you always wanted to without the pressure of well-meaning family and friends. And sometimes, after all of the parties and socializing and day trips to festive locations, you just want to relax and bask in the lights of your own Christmas tree.

If you don't feel like glamming up to face the masses, fear not! Your cozy slippers, robe, and flannel blanket are there for you. Christmas comes at a time when night falls early and chill creeps under the door. If you need to hibernate, you are more than welcome to do so. Whatever makes you feel festive, from cookies to cocoa to being alone, embrace those things. And remember, home at Christmas can also be more than one place. Home is transient. It may be a dorm room or a hotel room on a business trip with a small tree on the bureau. Home can mean carrying someone or some*thing* (like a tradition) with you wherever you go. But wherever home is, you deserve Christmas within it.

If you *are* in your own home, though, and you would love to host guests at Christmas, don't let worrying about making your place perfect for the season isolate you. Remember, Christmas has never demanded perfection. After all, a virgin girl and her betrothed traveled many miles, the mother to be on the back of a donkey, only to be turned away from every respectable establishment until they found shelter in a lowly stable. Away from home or cozy within its walls, imperfect is the heart of authenticity, and the moment we allow ourselves to be authentic, we offer the purest form of love: our true selves.

Customized VIEWING LIST

No matter where home is, though, is there anywhere quite like it at Christmas? I don't think so, especially if we can experience a few cherished traditions and even be with those we love most. Each movie below is like a warm hug and will make you wistful for Christmases of time past and the home and locations you might sometimes have taken for granted.

- *Coming Home for Christmas:* A young woman is given the opportunity to manage an upscale estate before its sale, in the process giving its owners one last memorable Christmas there. But she doesn't bet on falling in love with one of them.
- *The Christmas Ornament:* A widow finds Christmas traditions difficult after the loss of her husband, but an ornament from a shop owner and the magic that follows changes her mind about the season.
- *Sweet Mountain Christmas:* A country star heads home for a planned brief holiday, but a snowstorm keeps her there far longer than anticipated and reunited with an old sweetheart.
- *Homegrown Christmas:* When tasked with organizing a high school Christmas dance, a former CEO and her high school sweetheart revisit the past and plan a festive future together.

- *Christmas in Evergreen:* A veterinarian wishes upon a snow globe for the most romantic Christmas in hopes of coaxing a proposal from a longtime beau. But when a handsome single dad and his daughter arrive, her plans change.
- *Rocky Mountain Christmas:* An interior designer returns to her family's ranch for the holidays, but the arrival of a movie star set on learning how to ride and wrangle changes her plans.

Christmas After the Passing of a Loved One

Home will look different after the passing of a loved one. In ***The Christmas Plan***, the heroine's young niece has difficulty carrying on traditions that remind her too deeply of her now-deceased parents.

- Allow yourself the grace to grieve. If everyone is decking the halls and you're wrapped up in a favorite sweater of a deceased loved one, don't take on the burden of expectation.
- Honor a loved one's memory by ensuring their Christmas traditions are carried onward, yet tweak them if too many painful memories are stirred by carrying out those traditions the same way they did.
- Allow for a "memories" night, when favorite games are played, stories are told, photographs are shown, and videos are watched, all while honoring the one no longer present.

Holiday Table Tips on a Budget

Whether it's just you and your family or you're welcoming people into your home, use what you have around the house to create a festive atmosphere.

- Pine cones and a red-and-green ribbon around a candle holder or centerpiece can easily turn a year-round decoration into a festive one.
- Add red and green sprinkles to your sugar bowl.

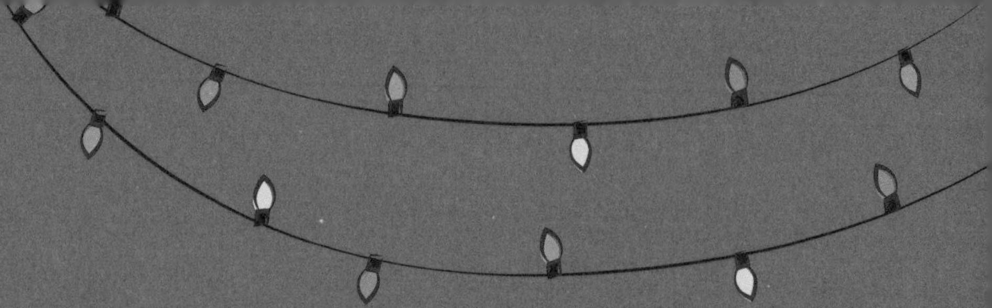

Imperfect is
the heart of
authenticity, and
the moment we
allow ourselves
to be authentic,
we offer the purest
form of love:
our true selves.

- A miniature bell-shaped or tree-shaped cookie cutter is perfect for making individual butter pats.
- Cinnamon sticks are a hostess's best friend during the holiday season. Either tie them together with red and green ribbons and serve them alongside a steaming mug of cider or tea or display them at each place setting.
- Have your kids create festive place mats for each setting, including the name of the diner. Hint: Painted handprints may be messy, but they make for wonderful reindeer antlers! And round plastic lids are an easy tracing tool to begin a wonderful snowman design! Glitter, stickers, and bows can help add a flourish to their creative designs.
- Inexpensive green and red shower curtain rings easily double as napkin rings when laying a Christmas table.
- Stenciled or stamped place cards make for an added festive touch.
- Place whole cranberries and plastic holly sprigs in your ice cube tray when you fill it with water for a perfect flourish to cold beverages.

Hometown Appreciation

Whether your current adult home or the location of your childhood home has the most precious Christmas memories, take time to immerse yourself in the magic of home—perhaps even making time for an experience you missed out on.

- Visit a locally owned shop you drive past during the everyday bustle and buy one locally made Christmas gift.
- Take a holiday-themed book to a local café and enjoy time to read.
- Attend midnight mass at a historic church you've passed but never been in.
- Visit with a music teacher, librarian, Sunday school teacher, or some other person from your past who significantly influenced you.

Make Home for Christmas Wherever You Are

My sister, Leah, has spent Christmas overseas in the United Arab Emirates (UAE) and in Africa, and she often found that Skyping home didn't have the desired effect—making her feel seasonally connected to home. Rather, it made her feel even farther away. So choosing how to create the feeling of home when you're away, wherever you are, takes some thought. Here are some ideas:

- Establish new holiday traditions with new friends so home takes on a different and temporary meaning.
- Give yourself the grace to celebrate Christmas on another day if it's too hard to celebrate it on December 25.
- Incorporate a local tradition into a gathering, such as a recipe or a song.

Make Reindeer Pretzels

INGREDIENTS

- Pretzel twists
- Chocolate candy (such as Hershey's Kisses or Cadbury or Ghirardelli squares)
- Small, round red candy (such as M&Ms)
- Store-bought candy eyeballs

Preheat the oven to 350°.

Place half of the pretzels on a lined baking sheet. Cut the remaining half in half for antlers.

Place the chocolate on top of the pretzels on the baking sheet, then place the sheet in the oven for 2 to 3 minutes or until the chocolate softens.

Remove from the oven and add a piece of red candy as a nose. Affix the antlers, add the eyes, and cool.

You can make as many or as few reindeer as you need.

Make Personal Hometown-Christmas-Lights-Tour Scoring Cards

One of my favorite family traditions is taking a drive around town with my parents just to look at Christmas lights and decorations. We choose the perfect clear night when snow has fallen and usually just after the Christmas Day rush. Whether you live somewhere with snow or without, you always have the opportunity to appreciate beautiful decorations!

Take along a few pieces of festive red and green paper and a pen. Then have each traveler rate the outside decorations they see (someone will have to keep score for the driver):

- **3 points:** outside lights around home and door
- **2 points:** inflatable snowman, reindeer, or other festive figure (Snoopy, anyone?) on the lawn
- **3 points:** festive music playing
- **2 points:** wreath on door
- **2 points:** festive adornment on house number plaque
- **3 points:** festive mailbox
- **1 point:** brilliantly decorated Christmas tree visible through a window
- **3 points:** personal preference for ____________________

Start a New TRADITION

Consider all of the people who may not be able to be home for Christmas, including emergency service workers, security guards, bus drivers, and anyone with a night shift that keeps them from a cozy Christmas Eve or Christmas Day. Arrange with management to take them packages with items like mittens or scarves, homemade Christmas goodies, and festive decorations in the spirit of bringing home to make their long holiday hours more bearable.

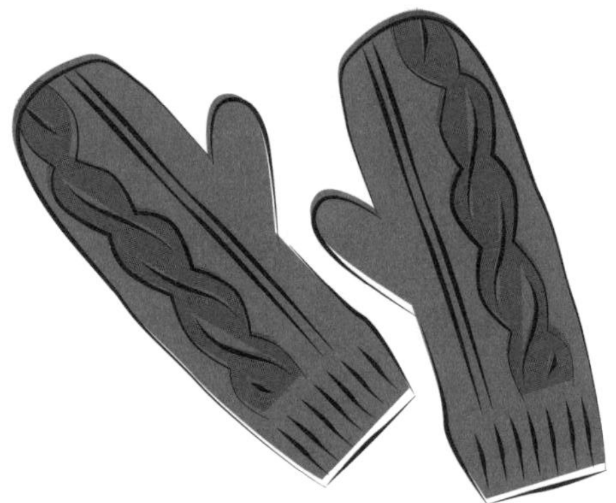

Festive FACTS

Christmas 1940 found Britons in the height of the Blitz (the shortened form of *Blitzkrieg*, which translates to "lightning war" in German) and under constant air raids and bombings. In fact, the bombing at the end of December 1940 (just before New Year) was so intense and destructive that Londoners deemed it "the Second Great Fire of London." With shortages and rations on everything from aluminum to stockings to paper, presents were often handmade and given from the heart. Favorite Christmas treats tasted less extravagant due to rations of sugar, butter, and fruit. While many were forced to spend Christmas Eve in bomb shelters rather than around a cozy tree, the sense of community in a time of despair and the improvisation of stories, carols, and games for children made for a memorable if changed celebration. The crypts and canteens under some of London's beautiful churches (such as St. Martin in the Field's just off Trafalgar Square) gave those homeless or wanting company a place to retreat for warmth and food.

The City Lover's Christmas

You're not supposed to leave. You're supposed to remember that it's Christmas, and anything is possible at Christmas.

CHRISTMAS AT PEMBERLEY MANOR

As a little girl living in a small town, I always wanted to move to the city. Now I've lived in Toronto for several years, and the bustle of the holiday season is one of my favorite aspects of city life.

Something about the holidays makes the large-city world grow smaller. With urban centers often a patchwork quilt of cultures and traditions, taking advantage of your city's broad and diverse background can make for a meaningful experience. This season, step out of your Christmas comfort zone by making time to learn about another culture. While Christmas is certainly the dominant holiday celebrated in North America during December, holidays like Hanukkah and Kwanzaa can teach us about festivities in other parts of the world. Use the privilege of living in the city to open your eyes to the world around you, and choose to make the many cultures, traditions, and people near you part of understanding the world you live in.

*This season,
step out of
your Christmas
comfort zone
by making
time to learn
about another
culture.*

Yet Christmas in the city can also seem overwhelming because it offers so very many wonderful things to do and see—concerts, outdoor ice skating, Christmas tree lightings, living nativities. You can also find holiday-themed menus, shopping pop-ups, and, of course, decorations everywhere. I sometimes found I just couldn't get to everything I wanted to do without squeezing each day of the season so much that I wasn't enjoying it. That's why I suggest using the last weeks of November to look over all the upcoming events and opportunities for the holidays and determine which ones you'll most relish. It's better to experience a few things with enough time to enjoy them than to make yourself too busy. After all, most of these events and opportunities are an annual tradition, so what you miss one year you can take in the next year.

City-Living Christmas Tips

You can't deck out your city apartment as you might a rambling old homestead, but you can make flourishes and touches that loan it a homey feeling.

- If you live in a complex with other people, meet to decide on joint outdoor decorations.
- If you can't share your public love of Christmas on your lawn or window, and if a huge tree just won't cut it, take Christmas with you and decorate your office or cubicle at work.
- If coworkers share your passion for decoration and management is in agreement, craft a Christmas corner in a popular

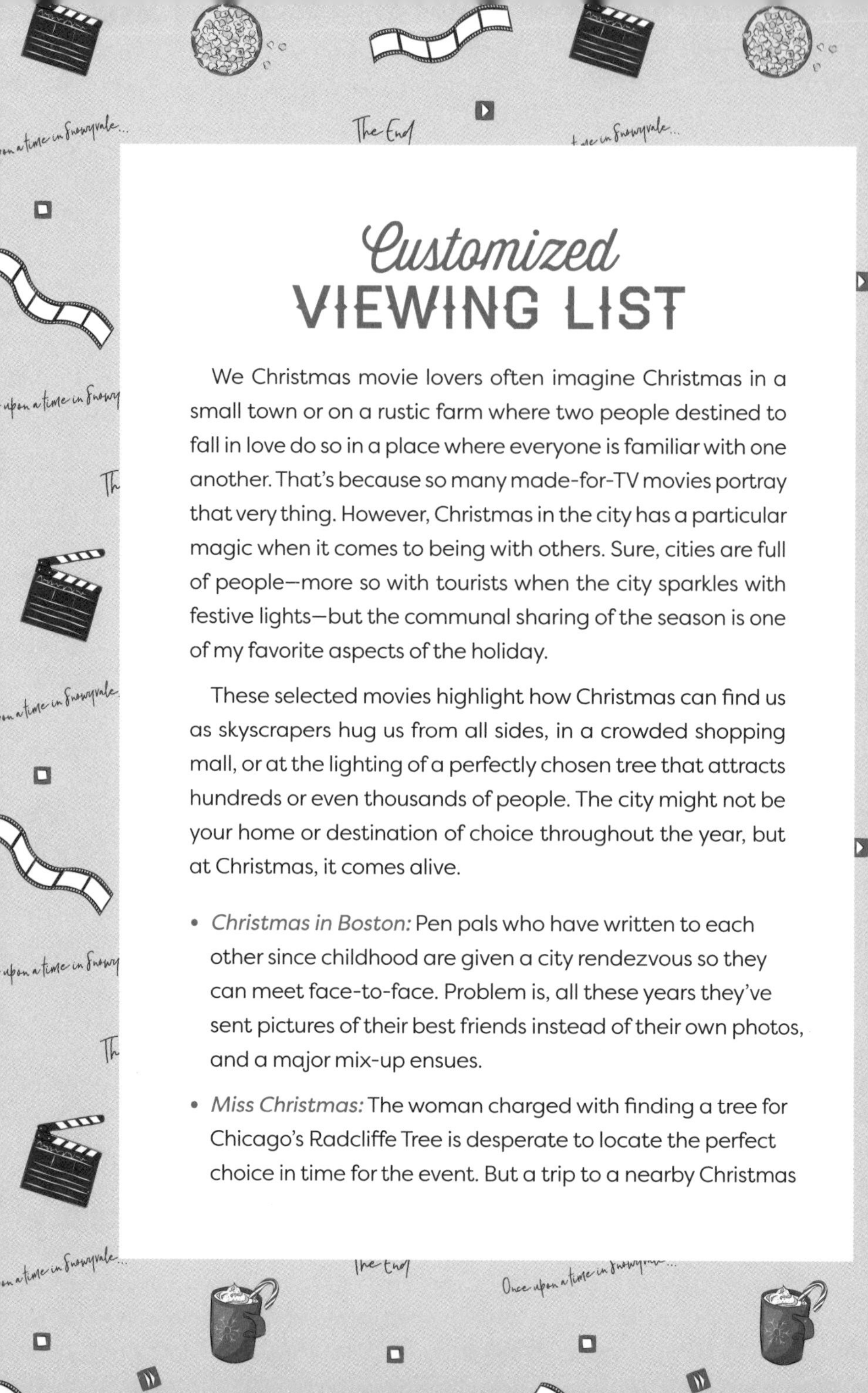

Customized VIEWING LIST

We Christmas movie lovers often imagine Christmas in a small town or on a rustic farm where two people destined to fall in love do so in a place where everyone is familiar with one another. That's because so many made-for-TV movies portray that very thing. However, Christmas in the city has a particular magic when it comes to being with others. Sure, cities are full of people—more so with tourists when the city sparkles with festive lights—but the communal sharing of the season is one of my favorite aspects of the holiday.

These selected movies highlight how Christmas can find us as skyscrapers hug us from all sides, in a crowded shopping mall, or at the lighting of a perfectly chosen tree that attracts hundreds or even thousands of people. The city might not be your home or destination of choice throughout the year, but at Christmas, it comes alive.

- *Christmas in Boston:* Pen pals who have written to each other since childhood are given a city rendezvous so they can meet face-to-face. Problem is, all these years they've sent pictures of their best friends instead of their own photos, and a major mix-up ensues.
- *Miss Christmas:* The woman charged with finding a tree for Chicago's Radcliffe Tree is desperate to locate the perfect choice in time for the event. But a trip to a nearby Christmas

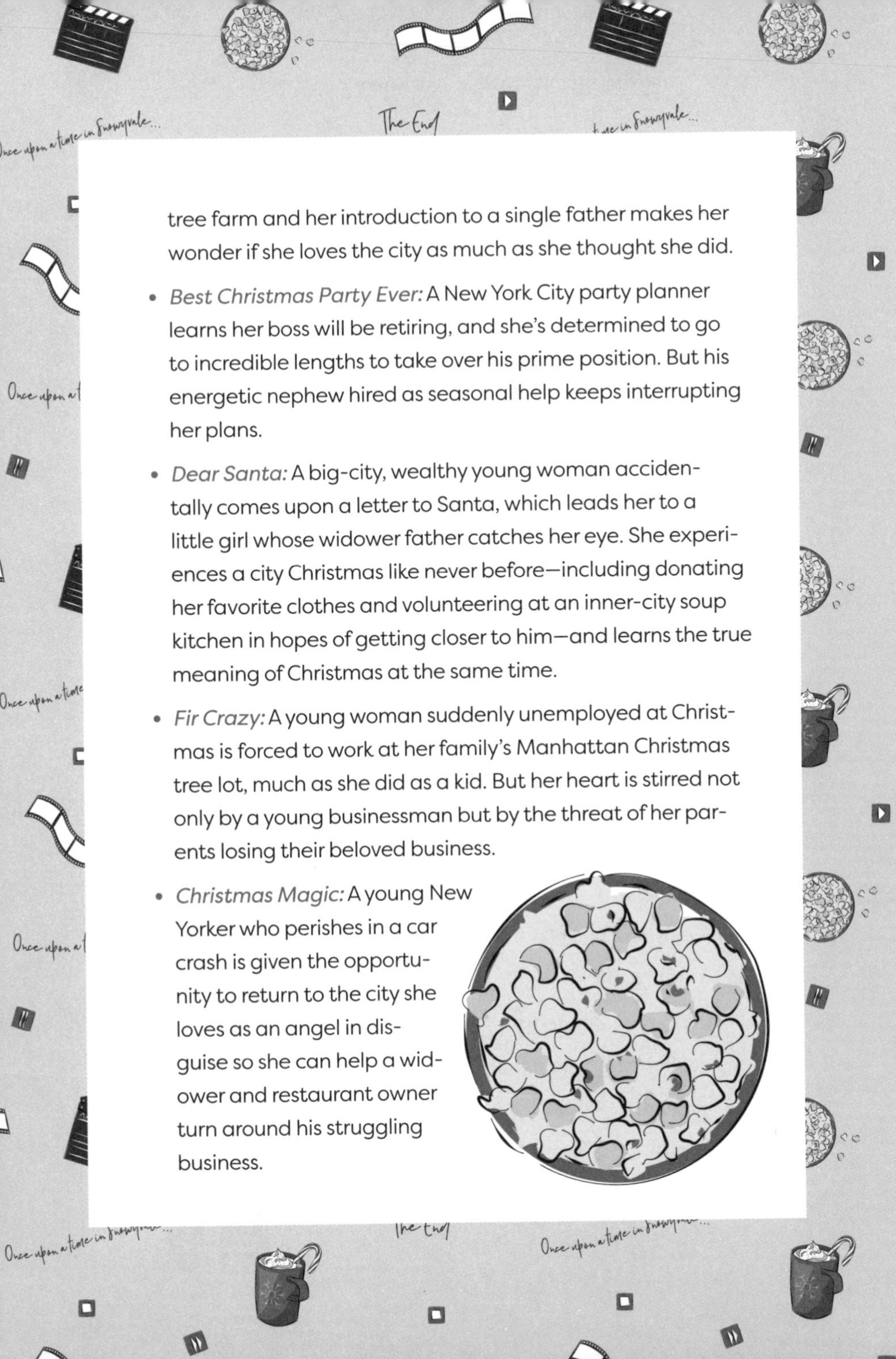

tree farm and her introduction to a single father makes her wonder if she loves the city as much as she thought she did.

- *Best Christmas Party Ever:* A New York City party planner learns her boss will be retiring, and she's determined to go to incredible lengths to take over his prime position. But his energetic nephew hired as seasonal help keeps interrupting her plans.
- *Dear Santa:* A big-city, wealthy young woman accidentally comes upon a letter to Santa, which leads her to a little girl whose widower father catches her eye. She experiences a city Christmas like never before—including donating her favorite clothes and volunteering at an inner-city soup kitchen in hopes of getting closer to him—and learns the true meaning of Christmas at the same time.
- *Fir Crazy:* A young woman suddenly unemployed at Christmas is forced to work at her family's Manhattan Christmas tree lot, much as she did as a kid. But her heart is stirred not only by a young businessman but by the threat of her parents losing their beloved business.
- *Christmas Magic:* A young New Yorker who perishes in a car crash is given the opportunity to return to the city she loves as an angel in disguise so she can help a widower and restaurant owner turn around his struggling business.

area near the coffee maker or kitchenette. Invite everyone to add items like homemade treats, the ingredients for festive punch, a small decorated tree, Christmas books, or a holiday pop-up.

- Feeling cramped and congested in the city? Most major cities have parks and golf courses that might provide a perfect afternoon escape in the form of sledding down their snowy hills. Better yet, see if your city has a toboggan run.

Take Yourself on a Christmas-City Date

I love to use the #TouristInMyOwnCity hashtag on Instagram. And the first time I used the term "on a date with my city" was a few Christmases ago when I was texting a friend. When she asked if I was busy, I told her I had plans—not with a person but with a place.

I woke up, donned my favorite festive colors—including a beanie hat with a pompom—and set out. I bought my favorite decadent beverage at a Starbucks, and then I started my city day.

Here are some suggestions for your Christmas city date:

- Stop at a few different subway stations not on your normal route to listen to the buskers play holiday tunes.
- Wander through a crowded mall without the intention of shopping. Rather, drink in a sense of the bustle and thrill.
- Visit the city hall tree.
- Unwind from all of the crowds with lunch at a café in a perfect people-watching spot.
- Take in a matinee of a Christmas movie or at a theater or attend a concert.
- Take advantage of the early darkness by wandering through the centers and squares where the sparkly lights are in their prime.
- Try to find local carolers in an open market. (Note: Some office buildings host holiday fairs of their own in their lobbies and foyers, so keep your eyes peeled for those.)
- Visit favorite buildings, churches, or landmarks to see how they sport their holiday colors.

Start a New TRADITION

Sometimes the city can seem like an overwhelming place. But I truly believe that even sprawling urban centers can be looked at as a collection of small towns if you divide them into the neighborhoods that give them character. Consider Christmas a time to make your world smaller by engaging in your neighborhood and even volunteering. Perhaps a nearby business needs help with a float for the Santa Claus parade. Does a local charity need someone to man a nearby donation kettle or a donation tree benefiting children? Christmas is a time to look at the world person by person, and even with crammed subways and bustling malls, there's always a chance for connection.

Festive FACTS

Few trees in the world are more iconic than the massive Christmas tree at Rockefeller Center in New York City. Every year it lights up as a worldwide symbol of holiday cheer. The tree is usually a Norway spruce ranging up to 100 feet tall, and its initial lighting is the subject of a live television broadcast featuring music and special guests.

The tradition of the tree began during the Depression, in 1931, when workers constructing the Rockefeller Center decorated a balsam fir with cranberries, tin cans, and paper garlands on Christmas Eve. In subsequent years, a tree became a tradition—albeit a much grander one—even leading to the opening of the equally iconic skating rink there in 1936. Throughout the decades since, the tree has reflected the current events of the time, such as adhering to blackout regulations during the Second World War and a patriotic display of red, white, and blue during the Christmas season following the 9/11 attacks.

The New Year Lover's Christmas

If happily ever after exists, then I want to find it.

ROYAL NEW YEAR'S EVE

New Year's can feel a tad bittersweet for me. The celebration not only announces the end of my favorite holiday but facing a brand-new, blank year feels a little daunting to me. And sometimes the prospect of throwing myself into the bustle of a big party can seem overwhelming after so many events at Christmas. But shh! I'll tell you a secret. This single city gal's favorite New Year's Eve includes catching up on whatever Masterpiece Theatre miniseries she missed during the year... with her parents during a visit home.

Whether you spend the months leading up to New Year's Eve searching for the perfect outfit and sparkly shoes for a party or you just fancy your pj's and some leftover eggnog or cider in the comfort of home, there is no right or wrong way to celebrate the new year.

If you don't feel like dressing up and going out or formally hosting family and friends but still want to make New Year's Eve a sparkly occasion, though, consider a stay-at-home party. Buy festive party horns and streamers to make it fun. Invite everyone to wear the one outfit they never seem to have the perfect occasion for or a favorite Halloween costume they're dying to wear again. Bring out that tiara or the big costume jewelry you're never brave enough to wear out. Put on those high, high heels you would trip over the moment you walked out the door but feel perfectly safe wearing them on the carpet of your rec room.

If you *are* going somewhere to celebrate, consider one last festive blowout! It's perfectly acceptable to bring out that sparkly red-and-green dress you didn't get the opportunity to wear because the office Christmas party was snowed out, and it's also a wonderful excuse to wear those snowman earrings or that jingle bell necklace one more time.

Ring in the new, yes, but hang on to all of your favorite Christmassy things for one more wonderful night!

Caring for Loose Ends

New Year's Day is a great time to get to activities or tasks you wish you had during the last year—or even during the recent holiday.

- What about that book you purchased but never cracked open? Try that recipe you clipped out of a magazine or pinned to Pinterest months ago. Does a craft or sewing project keep getting

Ring in

the new, yes,

but hang on to

all of your favorite

Christmassy

things for

one more

wonderful night!

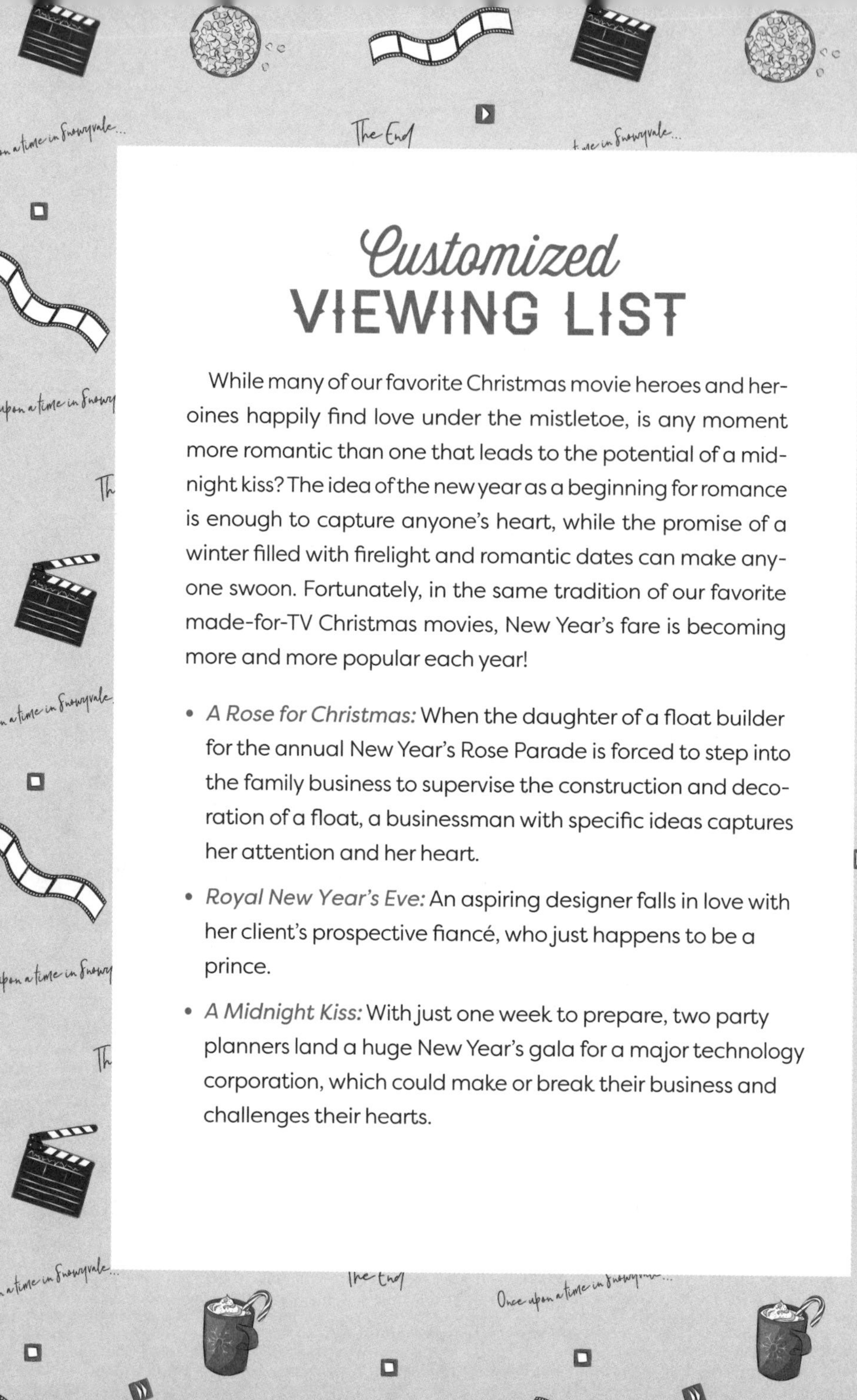

Customized VIEWING LIST

While many of our favorite Christmas movie heroes and heroines happily find love under the mistletoe, is any moment more romantic than one that leads to the potential of a midnight kiss? The idea of the new year as a beginning for romance is enough to capture anyone's heart, while the promise of a winter filled with firelight and romantic dates can make anyone swoon. Fortunately, in the same tradition of our favorite made-for-TV Christmas movies, New Year's fare is becoming more and more popular each year!

- *A Rose for Christmas:* When the daughter of a float builder for the annual New Year's Rose Parade is forced to step into the family business to supervise the construction and decoration of a float, a businessman with specific ideas captures her attention and her heart.
- *Royal New Year's Eve:* An aspiring designer falls in love with her client's prospective fiancé, who just happens to be a prince.
- *A Midnight Kiss:* With just one week to prepare, two party planners land a huge New Year's gala for a major technology corporation, which could make or break their business and challenges their hearts.

- *A New Year's Resolution:* When a morning show producer's resolution is to say yes more often, she doesn't count on a man who might not only have a story lead but hold her forever yes in his hands.
- *A Royal Winter:* A woman escapes on a European adventure to leave her troubles behind and finds herself in the middle of an unexpected fairy tale—castle and all!

sidelined? What about finally hanging those family photos you framed from summer vacation?

- Create a smorgasbord of Christmas leftovers still in your freezer or incorporate them into a recipe.
- Veg out. Maybe your New Year's Day should comprise comfy pajamas, slippers, and a binge-watch of all the made-for-TV Christmas movies you recorded on your DVR but didn't have a chance to enjoy.
- Give each member of your family the grace of allowing them to care for their own loose ends on their own schedule. If you usually serve lunch and dinner at a certain time, assemble buffet-type snacks or a make-your-own sandwich station instead.

Make Resolutions Fun

Some New Year's resolutions can create a lot of unnecessary stress. With fresh weight loss ads and gym membership commercials launching with the expectation that people should start reinventing themselves the moment the clock strikes midnight, the big day can certainly be a sobering end to a fun and meaningful week or two of Christmas celebrations. Depending on where you live, January can also be bleak. But while the dark of winter can be a prime time for sadness, carrying some holiday cheer into the winter months can prolong a cheerful outlook.

- If you'll just be returning from an enjoyable Christmas vacation or visit with loved ones, make plans with friends in advance of your homecoming to keep that festive feeling going.
- Do you ever feel that all of the socializing crammed from Thanksgiving through New Year's leaves large gaps between get-togethers the rest of the year? Put a stop to the vague "Let's make sure to get together in the new year" once and for all. Resolutions to combat this tendency could include a girls' night when the made-for-TV winter wedding and Valentine movies begin or reuniting for a Christmas in July party.
- New Year's resolutions might mean incorporating more joy in your life. For example, resolve to make one day trip to a fun, new place every month (maybe a museum, an art gallery, or a theater for a matinee performance). Or to try a new and challenging recipe once a week and invite someone to share the result. Make a resolution to read at least one book a month—in a genre you truly enjoy—or to veg out one night a week, ordering food in and donning your most comfy socks.

Meaningful Resolution Checklist

Be intentional when considering a new resolution by first contemplating your answers to the following questions:

- Will doing this benefit others?
- Will it enhance my creativity?

- Will I learn something new?
- Will it be a worthwhile and lifelong investment?
- Will it bring me joy?
- Is it achievable, and, most importantly, is it sustainable?
- Will it improve my mind or quality of life? (Learning a new language, returning to a musical instrument abandoned since high school, or taking a trip in the new year are examples of resolutions that might accomplish this.)

Turkey Curry

1 large onion, peeled and cut into chunks
1 red bell pepper, cored, seeded, and cut into chunks
2 tsp. canola oil
3 cloves garlic, peeled
1 (1-inch) piece fresh gingerroot, peeled and quartered
1 jalapeno pepper, quartered and seeded
1 T. curry powder
1 tsp. ground coriander
1 cup low-sodium chicken broth
¼ cup coconut milk, unsweetened
1 ripe banana, sliced
2 cups cooked turkey meat, diced

1 cup peas

¼ cup fresh cilantro, chopped

1½ T. fresh lime juice

¼ tsp. salt

¼ tsp. freshly ground pepper

Place the onion and red pepper in a food processor and pulse just until they're chopped. Heat the oil in a Dutch oven over medium heat. Add the onion-pepper mixture and cook, stirring until it's soft, 5 to 7 minutes.

Meanwhile, return the work bowl to the processor. With the motor running, drop the garlic, ginger, and jalapeno through the feed tube and process until they're finely chopped.

Add the garlic mixture to the onions, along with the curry powder and coriander. Cook, stirring, until fragrant, about 2 minutes. Add the chicken broth, coconut milk, and banana. Bring the mixture to a simmer, reduce heat to low, and then cover and simmer, stirring occasionally, for about 10 minutes.

Mash the banana to incorporate it into the sauce. Add the turkey, peas, cilantro, and lime juice and simmer until heated through, about 5 minutes. Season with salt and pepper.

Yields 4 servings

Start a New TRADITION

Treating the new year as a time of reflection, your family might benefit by recollecting both the highs and lows of the past year. Consider gathering with each member ready to share the following:

- one high
- one low
- one thing learned
- one thing still to learn
- one bad habit broken
- one good habit established
- one opportunity or adventure missed
- one opportunity or adventure taken

Festive FACTS

Without a doubt, the most important New Year's song is "Auld Lang Syne," an age-old tune that adapts lyrics from a poem by famed Scottish poet Robert Burns. Chances are, while everyone knows at least some of the words from their favorite movies or from New Year's Eve parties, many have no idea what *auld lang syne* means. In fact, some music historians call it the "song nobody knows but everybody sings." Written in 1788 and still popular at weddings and *ceilidhs* (Gaelic kitchen parties), "Auld Lang Syne" encourages singers to think about times past. It can be translated to mean *old long since; long, long ago; or for the sake of old times*.

The Best of the Rest

Yes! Yes I do! I like Christmas! I love Christmas!

A CHRISTMAS CAROL

Here are more great ideas for how you and your family can enjoy the most wonderful time of year.

Classic Christmas Movies

While made-for-TV Christmas movies are a personal reason I love the season, keep an eye out for more classic holiday film fare to watch as you snuggle near the television or your computer screen.

- ***White Christmas:*** Army buddies and now show partners go to extraordinary measures to save their beloved general's Vermont inn, complete with song and dance—and a chance at love.
- ***Holiday Inn:*** Two show entertainers fall in love with the same performer at a New England barn converted into a year-round holiday stage venue.
- ***Christmas in Connecticut:*** In this comedy, a city magazine

writer pretends to be a farm wife and mother for a series of stories before falling in love with one of her admirers.

- ***It's a Wonderful Life:*** The timeless tale of a man who thinks he's worth more dead than alive is given the gift of seeing the lives he's touched in his community, just in time for a joyous holiday.
- ***Miracle on 34th Street***: In charge of Macy's annual Thanksgiving parade in New York, a stressed-out single mother is determined her young daughter will never believe in Santa—until both a stranger-turned-friend and a love interest help change her mind.
- ***The Sound of Music:*** Though not technically a Christmas movie, this musical story of the von Trapp family featuring the gorgeous setting of late 1930s Salzburg, Austria, is a favorite movie-watching activity for many families during the holidays.

Santa, Is That You?

Movies about Santa and his world are always fun.

- ***Noelle:*** Kris Kringle's daughter is charged with finding her missing brother, Nick, when he disappears just before he's to take over the family business.
- ***Arthur Christmas:*** Santa's clumsy son sets out on a mission to deliver a misplaced present, and hilarity ensues.
- ***Klaus:*** A selfish postmaster is sent to the unhappiest place on

earth, only to learn the true meaning of selfless giving when he meets a humble toy maker.

- ***The Christmas Chronicles:*** Two siblings set out to capture Santa on camera and end up with more adventure than they bargained for.
- ***The Polar Express:*** A young boy who struggles with believing in Santa has the opportunity to travel to the North Pole on the magical Polar Express train.

A Christmas Carol

Check out these movies based on the 1843 novel *A Christmas Carol*.

- ***The Muppet Christmas Carol:*** Gonzo, Fozzie, Miss Piggy, and Kermit star in this retelling of the Dickens classic.
- ***Mickey's Christmas Carol:*** The more harrowing parts of the Dickens classic are made fun when Scrooge McDuck and Mickey Mouse are at the helm.
- ***The Man Who Invented Christmas:*** Charles Dickens has writer's block, and his financial situation demands a best-seller! It's a good thing Ebenezer Scrooge and friends show up in his writing chamber and start talking to him.
- Disney's ***A Christmas Carol:*** Brilliantly unique animation loans a lifelike feel to the Dickens story.

How to Celebrate Christmas in July

You may be sweltering in July, but in many towns and on many television stations, Christmas in July is a time-honored tradition. In my lakeside hometown, the weeks after Canada Day produce boats lit with festive twinkle lights and the appearance of Santa while Christmas music blares over the speakers on the boardwalk. On television, some of your favorite Christmas-movie-producing networks roll out a few holiday movies just to satiate your appetite amid the long wait for their usual late-October, Christmas-movie launch. If you can't fathom the interminable wait between July and December, here are a few suggestions for a sunny summer Christmas:

- Save a package of Christmas-blend coffee in the freezer and pull it out for festive iced coffee in the summer.
- Eggnog might not be widely available on grocery store shelves in summer months, so make do with alternatives, such as cranberry spritzers. You can even brighten up ice cubes with whole cranberries and plastic holly sprigs.
- Peppermint, ginger, and cinnamon flavorings are available year-round in the baking section of your grocery store, as are red and green sprinkles. Have fun with a little Christmas baking five months out from the real deal.
- Often, it doesn't take much to set the Christmas mood in July. Focus on four simple things rather than going so far out that

Keep an eye out for more classic holiday film fare to watch as you snuggle near the television or your computer screen.

you become overwhelmed. Choose, for example, one Christmas food, one Christmas decoration, one Christmas song, and one Christmas movie.

- Host a Christmas-themed potluck, encouraging guests to contribute to the summer event with their favorite December goodies.

How to Say "Merry Christmas" in Ten Different Languages

You can use Google Translate to hear how to pronounce these greetings.

1. French: *Joyeux Noel*
2. German: *Frohe Weinachen*
3. Spanish: *Feliz Navidad*
4. Italian: *Byon Natale*
5. Dutch: *Vrolijk Kerstfeest*
6. Czech: *Vesele Vanoce*
7. Romanian: *Cracuin Fericit*
8. Swahili: *Krismasi Njema*
9. Portuguese: *Feliz Natal*
10. Swedish: *God Jul*

Christmas Movie Bingo

Our favorite Christmas movies provide a canvas we want to return to again and again. Look for some of your favorite movie tropes as you play Christmas movie bingo.

CHRISTMAS TREE FARM	MALL SANTA	ICE SKATING	HOT CHOCOLATE	SLEIGH RIDE
NUTCRACKER PERFORMANCE	OUTDOOR CAROLING	TOWN CHRISTMAS TREE LIGHTING	ICE SCULPTURE CONTEST	BAKING COOKIES
GRANDFATHERLY CHARACTER WHO MIGHT BE SANTA	TOBOGGANING	FREE SPACE	BAKING COMPETITION	SLIPPING ON ICE
HOLIDAY BALL	SNOWBALL FIGHT	SALVATION ARMY BELL RINGER	TOWN TOY FACTORY IS SAVED	TRAVELERS STRANDED IN SNOWSTORM
CITY CHRISTMAS PARTY	REUNITED WITH HIGH SCHOOL SWEETHEART	PRINCE IN DISGUISE	CHRISTMAS PARADE	MISTLETOE

Mix and Match for Your Own Holiday Romance

I imagine you love holiday movies as much as I do, so maybe you'll want to use the following mix-and-match activity as a conversation starter at a holiday party or during a Christmas gift exchange with your girlfriends. Or perhaps you'll want to read these options aloud at an office Christmas luncheon and make it a game. Whether during the "intermission and snack procuring" part of a double-header girlfriend movie-watching party (a *fantastic* idea) or just to dream about on your own, make your Christmas sparkle with the romance of your own holiday movie adventure!

TITLES

- ***A Kiss for Christmas***
- ***The Mistletoe Prince***
- ***Her Holiday Wish***
- ***City Christmas Lights***

LOCATIONS

- Pine Cone, Virginia
- Santa Falls, Iowa
- St. Clair's Department Store, Boston
- The Kingdom of Fandalasia

HOLIDAY HEROINES

- *Melody Kringle:* Junior editor by day and knitter by night, Melody is heartbroken when her boyfriend, Chad, breaks off their engagement. Now she isn't sure if she should even go home for Christmas. What will her family think when at the ripe old age of 29 she's still without a marriage prospect, especially just before the holiday high school reunion?
- *Holly Gold:* Holly dreams of a fairy-tale romance, but after being downsized at her company's firm, she's forced to work as a happy Christmas department store elf over the holiday. (Don't worry. She has enough in her savings to still afford that big one-bedroom apartment in the middle of the city.)
- *Ivy St. Nicholas:* Vice president of Currier and Ives Marketing, Ivy hasn't been home to her small town for Christmas in years, choosing instead to wear perfectly creased pants and date her job.
- *Merry Evergreen:* A corporate Christmas planner who is dying for the chance to prove herself at a huge holiday party, secretly dreams of illustrating a children's book.

HOLIDAY HEROES

- *Nicholas St. Clair:* Nicholas is the son of the St. Clair empire set to inherit several department stores. Having just returned from a trip to Everest, he's assigned by his father to revamp the toy sales at the flagship store on Washington Street in Boston.
- *Blake Foster:* Blake is a single widowed dad and owner of a struggling Christmas tree farm. The lease on his farm might not be renewed if he fails to show property developers a 15 percent sales increase by December 26.
- *Travis Holt:* Travis is a former high school quarterback star and NFL hopeful whose dreams were smashed by an untimely injury. Now coaching high school football, he's in a loveless relationship and dying to find the true meaning of Christmas again.
- *Hunter Tomlinson:* Also known as His Royal Highness Hunter von Lichstein the Third, heir to the throne of Fandalasia, Hunter has no interest in the crown but knows it's his duty. After his father's death, his mother, the queen, grants him one final Christmas wish—a Stateside Christmas. She has two

conditions: He must not reveal his identity, and he must return in time for the royal Christmas Day ball.

HOLIDAY MEET-CUTES

A meet-cute is a film term describing the fated and memorable first meeting between the two leads of the film.

- Our heroine is shopping with her adorably precocious niece and accidentally runs over his expensive patent leather shoe with her shopping cart.
- She starts talking to her coworker about how difficult she's heard the CEO of the company whose event she's planning is, not noticing the coworker is motioning that he's right behind her.
- Hero and heroine reach for the last Frosty cupcake at the same time.
- He's lost and looking for directions, and as they both consult an app on his phone, she realizes he isn't just on the wrong street but in the wrong neighborhood. It's up to her to direct him. (Bonus points if they get lost together on the way.)

Make your

Christmas

sparkle with the

romance

of your own

holiday movie

adventure!

HOLIDAY ROMANTIC DATES

They've had their meet-cute and a few charming spats that never turned into actual arguments as our heroine navigates the attraction she tries but fails to hide. Now she gets to know her soul mate one-on-one.

- He brings her peppermint hot chocolate, and then they ramble together through the pines of a rustic Christmas tree ranch.
- They enjoy an impromptu diner run after she finds a gift for his grandmother, where they share French fries and milk shakes just like they did in high school. He remembers her favorite order perfectly.
- They bake midnight Christmas cookies after a long, caffeinated session of rehearsals for the high school Christmas concert.
- She introduces him to the American magic he's missing living in that faraway European country so that he never wants to leave: hot dogs, the city Christmas tree, a matinee of ***Elf***, a karaoke sing of Taylor Swift's Christmas album, and apple pie from the diner everyone knows.

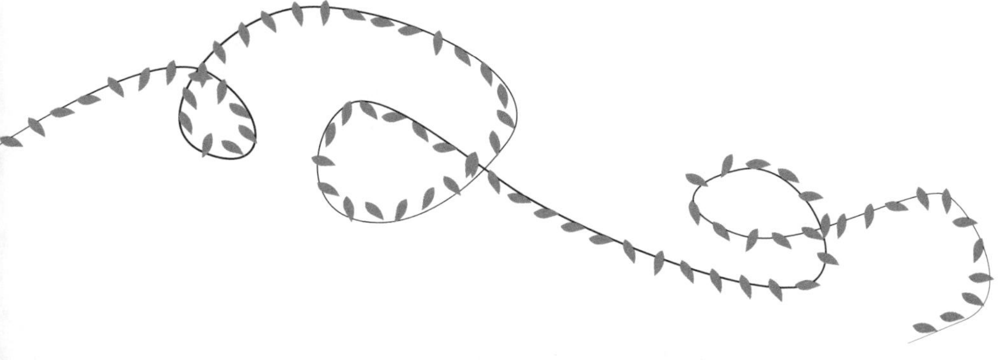

THE END-OF-MOVIE HOLIDAY KISS

It's two minutes before the credits will roll, and our heroine is finally given the opportunity to steal a romantic moment with the man of her Christmas dreams. Do the two of them smooch...

- at the town gazebo that wasn't torn down to build a high-rise after all (thank heavens)?
- under the largest pine on the recently saved Christmas tree ranch?
- on the balcony of a royal palace complete with turrets, flags, and parapets?
- in the now-deserted Santa's Toy Shop of a large department store?
- as the high school marching band practices "Deck the Halls" on the empty football field just as a whimsical snow begins to fall?

A Festive Taste of Romance

While I don't recommend asking a friend to pose as your boyfriend for that hometown holiday party or reunion you would otherwise attend alone (only to fall in love with him in the process), I do think Christmas can be a fun time to take a chance. Maybe finally say yes to the offer of a friend to set you up with her visiting cousin. Or think about opening an online dating account or even going to a Mix and Mingle event, a singles' dinner, or a speed dating opportunity.

One caution: While grabbing at the opportunity to enjoy new

experiences over the holidays is fun, remember that what we see in made-for-TV Christmas movies is a fairy-tale escape. Also, for most of us, making a lifelong commitment takes more than a week and a holiday engagement.

Remember that romance can have a broader meaning. While our modern definition includes what we see in our favorite movies when two people fall in love, it can also refer to any experience, emotion, or feeling that helps us engage in art, beauty, and philosophy. If you choose to be a romantic in this way, you still have a great romance ahead of you as the world truly sparkles at Christmastime.

How to Find the Perfect Holiday Guy at Christmas

1. Frequent Christmas tree lots and inexplicably show up to purchase the one he and his orphaned niece are contemplating. (Bonus points if the tree has a Charlie Brown flair and this guy offers to help you haul it to your car.)

2. Accidentally set off your smoke alarm while baking gingerbread cookies so that a fully decorated fire truck pulls up to your house. (Bonus points if the dashing firefighter who sweeps you to safety has affixed holly sprigs to his helmet.)

3. Volunteer to play the piano at the children's Christmas pageant directed by the winsome single dad who holds auditions. (Bonus points if you begin singing a favorite carol and he joins in perfect harmony, accompanying you both with his guitar.)

4. Cater a holiday event for the uptight CEO of a tech start-up company. (Bonus points if you bicker over canapés before learning that he has a heart of gold and donates most of his profits to orphanages.)
5. Offer to tutor a diplomat's daughter while they visit over the holidays. (Bonus points if the diplomat turns out to be a European prince in disguise.)
6. Step into a struggling toy store owned by a handsome single man to buy your niece the perfect Christmas gift. (Bonus points if you end up cohosting a fundraiser to help the owner/woodcarver who needs to save his shop by New Year's Eve.)
7. Slip on the ice at the outdoor city skating rink, not hurting anything but your pride but near an array of potential male saviors. (Bonus points if the handsome, broad-shouldered man who rescues you just happens to be a former hockey player who left his multi-million-dollar corporation to help his parents save their Christmas cookie factory.)
8. Submit a strongly worded letter to the local newspaper protesting the development of high-rise condos where the historical Mistletoe Bridge has welcomed couples since the town's founding—but only if the editor is handsome and single. (Bonus points if the editor writes you back, beginning a weeklong correspondence that turns into love.)

9. Take a dance class with a girlfriend at the community center where single men also want to learn to dance. (Bonus points if your waltzing partner spins you straight from the floor and off to his family's poinsettia farm for the holidays.)

10. Work as a barista at a café that serves Cinnamon Swirl and Gingerbread Frosting lattes and wait for a well-dressed businessman to come in and order a coffee straight black so you can change his mind and inspire his Christmas spirit. (Bonus points if you correctly spell his name on the cup, thereby impressing him all the more.)

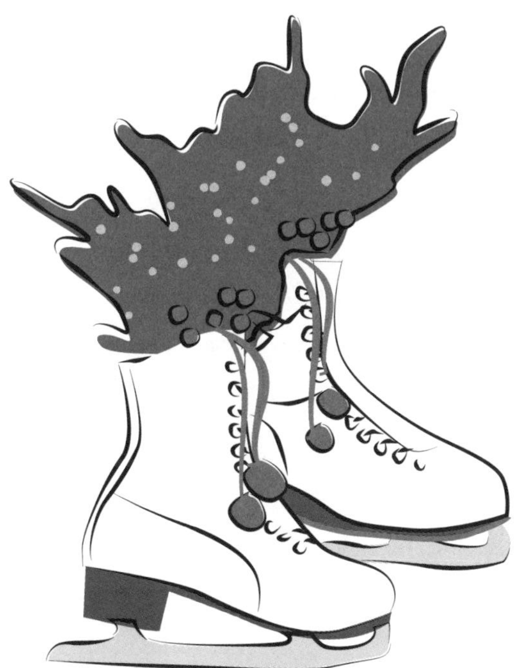

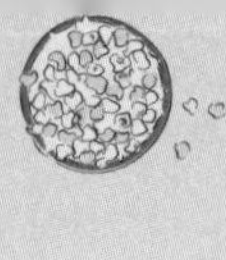

Start a New TRADITION

Make it a point to live out Christmas all year long. While garlands and decorated trees might not adorn your neighborhood shops or mall most months, the spirit of Christmas can be tapped and encouraged anytime.

- If you're on summer vacation in a town or city with a year-round Christmas store, start your décor shopping. In hopes of just such an opportunity, take along a list of desired items you started at the end of the last holiday season. You might also discover an irresistible item you won't find where you live, a gift for either yourself or for another lover of all things Christmas.
- Intentionally think about how you can continue the best parts of Christmas from January through November. This might mean volunteering at a food bank, offering to do your elderly neighbor's shopping, or reconnecting with an old family friend or distant relative.
- Pull out the boxes of Christmas cards you purchased on sale directly after the holiday to inspire you. You might not be ready to address them and write your greetings, but you can update your list of recipients and ensure your address book is up-to-date as well.

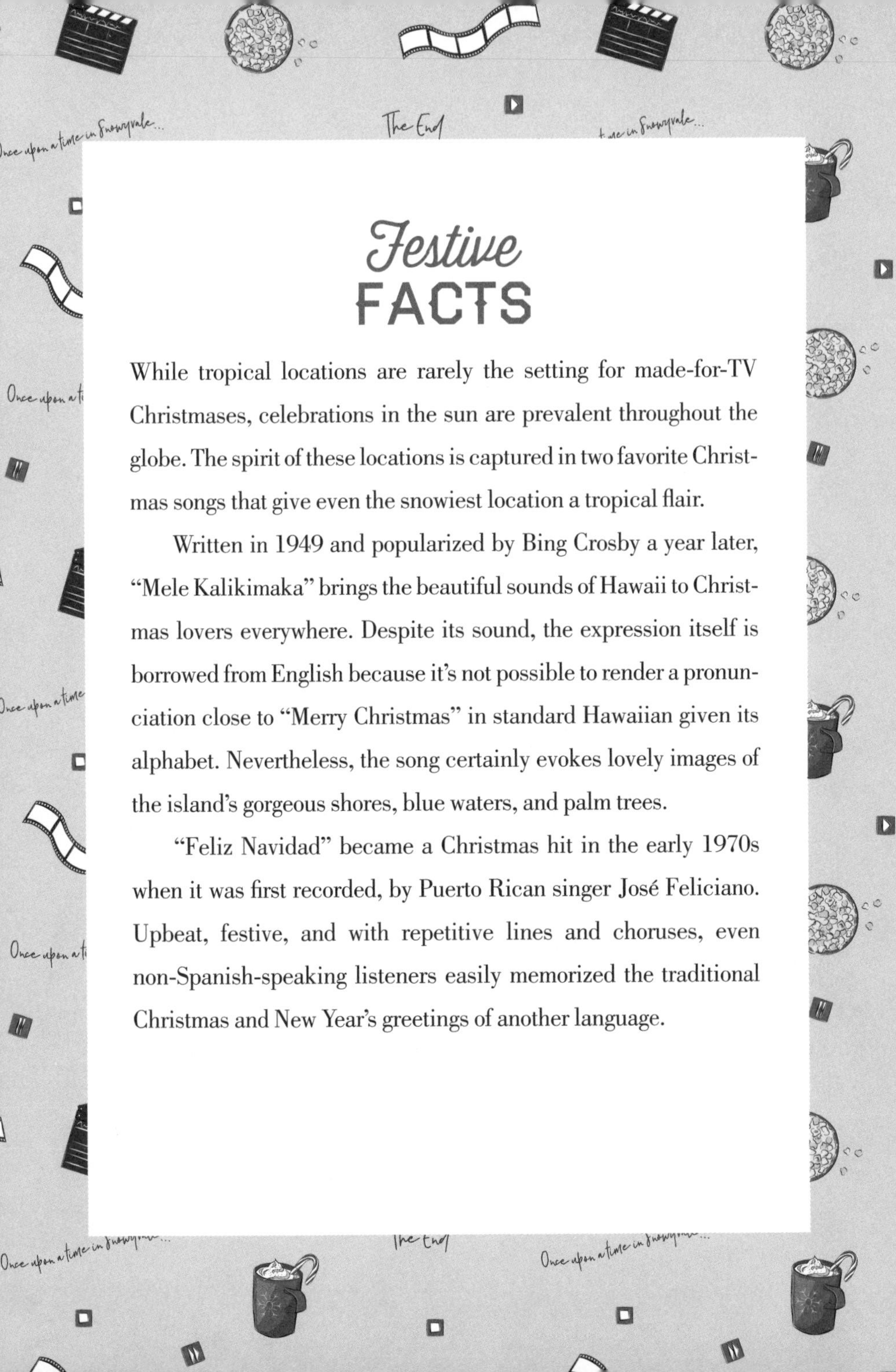

Festive FACTS

While tropical locations are rarely the setting for made-for-TV Christmases, celebrations in the sun are prevalent throughout the globe. The spirit of these locations is captured in two favorite Christmas songs that give even the snowiest location a tropical flair.

Written in 1949 and popularized by Bing Crosby a year later, "Mele Kalikimaka" brings the beautiful sounds of Hawaii to Christmas lovers everywhere. Despite its sound, the expression itself is borrowed from English because it's not possible to render a pronunciation close to "Merry Christmas" in standard Hawaiian given its alphabet. Nevertheless, the song certainly evokes lovely images of the island's gorgeous shores, blue waters, and palm trees.

"Feliz Navidad" became a Christmas hit in the early 1970s when it was first recorded, by Puerto Rican singer José Feliciano. Upbeat, festive, and with repetitive lines and choruses, even non-Spanish-speaking listeners easily memorized the traditional Christmas and New Year's greetings of another language.

CONCLUSION

Perfect? Or Brilliantly Imperfect?

A true act of goodwill always sparks another.

KLAUS

As I said in the homebody chapter, one wonderful thing about Christmas is that it never insists on perfection. That's good, because sometimes parts of the season don't go as perfectly as planned. We can be disappointed, like being forced to order pizza delivery after canceling an eagerly anticipated reservation at a fancy restaurant because of an approaching snowstorm. Or we can simply experience a change in plans, like running into an old friend while shopping, sparking a last-minute lunch date. Or stepping into the church Christmas pageant when an angel comes down with a cold.

Maybe, then, your picture-perfect Christmas is actually imperfect. And that's okay, because there's no right or wrong way to celebrate the season. It can be *brilliantly imperfect*—a hodgepodge that beautifully colors outside the lines, like the buffet with leftovers from turkey to cheese to apple pie two days after Christmas. Even if an unexpected chance to spend time with an old friend delays your Christmas shopping, think of the opportunity as a blessing. And if your plans fall through, your turkey never thaws, you burn the cookies, or you accidentally buy a gift the recipient already has, it doesn't matter. Christmas won't let you down. It will meet you wherever you are and be whatever you need it to be.

For some people, though, Christmas can be a challenge, a bittersweet time no matter their plans. It can remind them of those they've lost or of happier times—before their lives rerouted and changed. Other times it's a reminder of what they don't have or expectations they couldn't live up to. But at its core, Christmas is a season that can bring out the best in the world, the best in us all. We can focus on generosity, smile at fellow shoppers, and pay it forward in the Starbucks line. We might witness acts of goodwill, random or planned, which as Klaus says in the Netflix film bearing his name, always spark others.

This brings me to our made-for-TV Christmas movies. One of the moments I realized their widespread popularity was on an international flight, where several Christmas movies were options for onboard entertainment. But why are they so popular? I think when we consider the travails and triumphs of an uneven year in a world burdened by war, poverty, and uncertainty, it makes sense that we would want to steal into channels that portray happy and meaningful celebrations of Christmas for a few months of the year.

But the Christmas movies we love are not as perfect and pristine as they look. They include moments of vulnerability and characters who reflect on how Christmas can change them. Also, though they're brilliantly designed and feature good-looking actors on sets that make the season look ideal, we may not be able to emulate the gorgeous gift-wrapping, and our own tree may not sit as if ushered in from a magical wood. But we can still embrace our love for the films—perhaps a love inspired by our affection for tradition and the remembrances of Christmases past. In this way, they can be an encouragement and jump-start new Christmas traditions of our own.

Remember this, though: Our Christmas celebrations might not be as picture-perfect as our beloved Christmas movies, but Christmas can still be the best time of the year when they're *brilliantly imperfect*.

The End

Acknowledgments

Writing this book was an absolute joy. My favorite season is Christmas, and the opportunity to share my love of it brings a smile to my face.

Thanks to my agent, Bill Jensen, who put up with my super-excited, talk-a-mile-a-minute phone calls. Thank you for always believing in me—but also for chats that start with book business and inevitably end up with an hour of Mozart talk.

Ruth Samsel, you are a constant champion and dear friend. Thank you for always believing in my ideas—and in me—and for your creative spirit and brilliant insight.

Heather Green, I loved your good-humored approach and patience with me.

Kim Moore, my dream is that we'll someday sit together and watch a few Christmas movies while drinking cocoa and chatting. You are a delight to partner with on any project.

Laura Bean, you are talented and optimistic and a true wonder! Thank you, thank you!

The entire team at Harvest House, I'm so excited to continue to journey with you. I love you all, and I feel such a part of the community.

Allison Pittman, Melanie Fishbane, and Sonja Spaetzel, I would rather talk about Christmas movies with you than…well, do most anything else.

And for my family—Kathleen and Gerald McMillan, Jared and Sarah (and, of course, Maisie, Ellie, and Kieran), and Ken and Leah—my Christmases are always better than picture-perfect because they're *ours*.

About the Author

Rachel McMillan is the author of the Herringford and Watts mysteries, the Three Quarter Time series of contemporary romances set in opulent Vienna, the Van Buren and DeLuca mysteries, and *The London Restoration*.

Her first works of nonfiction, *Dream, Plan, and Go* and *Dream, Plan, and Go Adventure Journal*, released in 2020.

Rachel lives in Toronto, Canada, and she believes she deserves an honorary degree in Christmas movies.

You can connect with her via:

Facebook: **@rachkmc1**

Twitter: **@rachkmc**

Pinterest: **@rachkmc**

Instagram: **@rachkmc**

RACHEL McMILLAN

dream

plan

& go

a travel guide to inspire your independent adventure

ARTWORK by LAURA BEAN

A Great Big World Is Waiting for You Out There—Go Find It!

Have you been putting off that trip of a lifetime hoping for a special someone to accompany you? Do you find yourself getting bored with the same old girls' weekends? Are you hesitant to step out of your comfort zone, plan a solo vacation, pack your bags, and just go?

From pastries in Vienna to becoming a tourist in your own town and all points in between, this travel memoir and guidebook will inspire you to seek romance and adventure on your own terms. You will also get practical advice on how to stay safe while traveling single, create a budget, prepare and pack efficiently, and much more.

Chapter by chapter, you'll encounter creative ideas for excursions as well as historical insights into some of the most fascinating destinations around the globe, smart tips for savvy sojourning, and journal jump-starts to encourage deeper reflection Grab with both hands the confidence you need to embrace new experiences both home and abroad. You deserve the chance to discover the joy of being your own best company—this book will show you how!

dream, plan, & go

Adventure Journal

with helpful travel tips from

RACHEL McMILLAN

ARTWORK *by* LAURA BEAN

"The purpose of life is to live it, to taste experience to the utmost, to reach out eagerly and without fear for newer and richer experience."

– ELEANOR ROOSEVELT

Celebrate your passion for travel as you record your adventures in this one-of-a-kind journal. So much more than just blank space for you to write in, you'll encounter inspired ideas for excursions both big and small, helpful tips for savvy sojourning, and creative prompts to jump-start your journaling.

When you dream, plan, and go, you'll gain greater confidence to venture out of your comfort zone and open yourself to new, exciting experiences, and you will learn more about yourself as you explore.

There's a great big world waiting for you—go and find it!

HARVEST HOUSE PUBLISHERS
EUGENE, OREGON